MOMENTS OF KNOWING

By the same Author:

MOMENTS OF KNOWING

*Some Personal Experiences Beyond
Normal Knowledge*

by

ANN BRIDGE

HODDER AND STOUGHTON

Copyright © 1970 by Ann Bridge

First Print 1970

ISBN 0 340 12889 5

Printed in Great Britain for Hodder and Stoughton Limited,
St. Paul's House, Warwick Lane, London, E.C.4. by
The Camelot Press Ltd., London and Southampton

Introduction

When I was young the expression "Extra-Sensory Perception" had not yet been coined; or if it had been, it was not in common use. People with Highland blood, or Highland kinsfolk, spoke as a natural thing of "second sight"; inexplicable communications came to be called "telepathy" or "telepathic communication"; people who, with greater or less success, foretold the present or the future from cards or tea-leaves, were known, oddly, as "fortune-tellers"—gypsies were rightly considered to be outstandingly good at this. Truth-telling dreams are of course as old as the Bible, and from Old Testament times onwards were regarded as one means of communication between the Divinity and the human race. I imagine that all these phenomena would now be included under the general heading of extra-sensory perception. I have no scientific knowledge of the subject. I am merely a person who frequently has, when awake, inexplicable "knowings", as I prefer to call them, of events taking place at a distance; and, in dreams, am informed, sometimes uncomfortably, of facts of which I can have no knowledge by normal means. Many I have forgotten; of none have I any written or oral evidence, for reasons which will be explained in their place. But since I began recalling my own experiences, and setting them down, along with those of others well known to me (of whose truthfulness I could have no doubts), I have come to realise that my own experience is by no means an isolated one. There is much more of this sort of thing going on in everyday life than most of us imagine; once one has admitted to a serious interest in extra-sensory perception, the most sober-sided people will come up with dreams and "knowings" of their own—often shyly hidden hitherto for fear of being laughed at. I myself believe that the capacity for such experience is to a greater or less extent common to the whole human race; more developed in some individuals than in others, but not in the least the monopoly of a "lunatic fringe".

What follows is an account, as accurate as I can make it, of some of these dreams and knowings—beginning with my own.

Contents

PART I

Personal Experiences

I

The Ascot Procession
(KNOWING)

1904

The first "knowing" that I remember occurred when I was about 12. We lived then on the outskirts of Windsor Great Park, where my sister Grace and I, escorted by a groom, rode every day of the week except Sundays—in the winter before lunch, in the summer after tea. The high spot of the summer rides for us was Ascot Week, when the King and Queen and their guests drove in open carriages from Windsor Castle to Ascot Heath and back, along the green rides of the Park; they always followed the same route, at exactly the same time, and by arriving early and posting ourselves judiciously, we could watch the whole procession pass from quite close to, and when the last carriage had gone, turn, gallop off at a tangent, come up to the route again a mile or so further on, and, bowing respectfully over our ponies' withers, see the beautifully-dressed company a second, or even a third time. It was, on any showing, a splendid sight—each carriage with three pairs of horses, a postillion in a dark blue velvet jockey-cap to each perfectly-matched pair: for Gold Cup days, the creams, on other days, the greys or the bays. We greatly admired the King, in his grey top-hat above his well-trimmed grey beard; still more Queen Alexandra, nearly always wearing some combination of mauve and chestnut-brown, the brown exactly matching the tightly-frizzed fringe above her lovely enamelled face. And, year after year, there were familiar figures among the guests—invariably Consuelo, Duchess of Marlborough, with her incredibly long neck, whose face somehow looked holy even under a picture hat; and the Portuguese Minister, the Marques de Soveral. He was considerably amused by our comings and goings, and being an ebullient person, clapped his hands vigorously when we drew up, panting a little, just in time to see the procession pass for the third time.

Naturally, we would not for worlds have missed this magnificent entertainment, and always set out in good time, perfectly happy to wait ten minutes or more at the first passing-place. To reach this we had to ride down a wooded slope not far from the Royal Chapel in the Park, and then proceed some three-quarters of a mile along an open ride running at right-angles to the royal route; the track down this slope was rough and stony, and we had to pay attention to our reins; the trees were so thick that one could see nothing of the open grassy expanse beyond.

On this occasion, riding down through the wood, I said to Grace—"Wouldn't it be funny if when we come out at the bottom we were to see the postillions' jockey-caps bobbing up and down over the grass?" Grace, as usual, told me brusquely not to be a fool; we were in heaps of time. We reached the foot of the slope and emerged from the trees—there, in the distance, we saw the dark-blue caps going up and down, up and down, above the fine heads of the grass. Indignant, feeling almost betrayed, we rode off to the second passing-place, where we were in time to see the whole procession from close to as usual.

This is, of course, the most trivial episode imaginable; it has no personal or telepathic content whatever. But what has always interested me was the extreme visual accuracy of this knowing. It would have required some complicated calculations with a theodolite, to know that from that precise spot, at the precise height of a child on horseback, all that would be visible of the long elaborate procession, more than half a mile away, would be the caps of the postillions, rising in their saddles to the movement of the trotting horses. No—the only possible explanation, it seems to me, is that at the moment when I spoke to Grace, time, for me, had somehow slipped, as it was to slip, later on, at Abbotsford. But that was in a dream; in Windsor Great Park I was broad awake.

(My sister Grace, like all the rest of my family, is dead, so no corroboration is possible.)

2

The Ladies Alpine Club Dinner
(DREAM)

1912

In 1911, while up in Scotland in a house taken for the shooting and fishing, we learned that my Father had lost practically all his money; he could allow each of his six daughters £50 a year, our previous dress-allowance, but no more—we should have to earn our own livings. This we proceeded to do. With my sisters Helen and Grace I settled down in a very small, very noisy and very cheap flat on the Fulham Road—Helen, who had an Oxford degree, got a rather good job in the Civil Service; Grace, who was ill, kept house for us, and I was taken on as Assistant Secretary to the Chelsea Branch of the old C.O.S., the Charity Organisation Society, which did such marvellous work for London's poor before the advent of the Welfare State. My hours were from nine-thirty to six-thirty, and I was paid twenty-three shillings a week. (When I went to be interviewed by the Committee they enquired, finally, if I wished to ask any questions on my own account? I said, "Yes, one—could I give up one week of my summer holiday, and instead take an afternoon and a morning off in mid-week, five or six times, in the winter?" Startled, the Chairman asked why? "To go to Hunt Balls," I said—at that time I could not imagine why this request produced such a sensation. In the event I went to my Hunt Balls *and* had my month's holiday; the Society was well named.)

A year or two before I had been made a member of the Ladies' Alpine Club—by 1910 I had had four good seasons, with guides, in the Alps, and had climbed a lot in Wales with Geoffrey Winthrop Young, George Mallory, and others; I had even made a new route up the Zermatt Weisshorn at the age of 19. Climbing was really the greatest thing in my life at that time; in London, the two great events of the year, for me, were the Alpine Club At Home at the men's old premises in Savile Row, and the Ladies Alpine Club annual dinner, which always took place in the Great Central Hotel. This was a large affair, 250 people at least; the Alpine Club came to it *en masse*, and the speech of the evening was always the one proposing the toast of "The Alpine Club", which one of the ladies had to make.

In the early autumn of 1912 I had influenza rather badly, and my kind Godmother, Eleanor Wood, invited me down to her comfortable seaside house in the Isle of Wight to get over it, and be spoiled and cosseted—I was made to rest every afternoon, and once on my bed, I always slept. During one of these afternoon sleeps I dreamt that I had been asked to propose the health of the Alpine Club at our forthcoming winter dinner; I agreed, and still dreaming, composed a speech. When I woke up I remembered it clearly, and wrote it down at once; I thought it fairly funny and rather good, and kept it. Back at work in London—in the Whitechapel Office of the C.O.S., now at the princely salary of thirty shillings a week—I was summoned, one foggy afternoon, to the telephone. It was the Secretary of the Ladies' Alpine Club—the Committee were holding a meeting to arrange the annual dinner, and they wished to know if I would agree to propose the health of the Alpine Club? (I learned later that the Committee felt that for the Club baby to make the main speech might be an amusing change.) I said yes, and asked about length—twelve to fifteen minutes, I was told. Seven or eight weeks later, in that huge room at the Great Central Hotel, I stood up and made the speech I had composed in a dream, at Ventnor, three months before.

On previous occasions I had noticed that the women speakers

were often, in fact usually, rather difficult to hear; on the way in I examined a big diagram of the tables with the names of those who were to sit at them. At the table furthest away from my place I saw, by good luck, the name of Claude Schuster, the Clerk to the Crown, and his wife; I sought out Lady Schuster and asked her to do me a favour. If, when I began to speak, she could not hear every syllable without the smallest effort, would she please raise her menu and move it to and fro; I would alter the pitch of my voice, and when she could hear perfectly, would she put it down? She kindly agreed. This seemed to me an elementary precaution: I had never spoken in public in my life, let alone in a huge room with 250 distinguished people, bishops and judges and civil servants and their wives, sitting listening. I had of course rehearsed the speech, for length, with Grace and Helen in our tiny sitting-room; but that told me nothing about audibility. Having arranged this, I sat down with Helen and my other guests, and enjoyed my dinner. When I began to speak, up came kind Lady Schuster's menu; but in a couple of sentences I had got my voice right; the menu went down again, and remained down.

A few days after the dinner I received a letter from the then head of the old Anglo-Persian Oil Company, forwarded from the Club; it read:

"Dear Madam, My friend Sir Martin Conway heard you make a speech at the Ladies' Alpine Club Dinner two nights ago. He knows that I have been seeking a personal private secretary for some time, without success, and he thinks you would probably fill the post admirably"—and went on to ask me to go and see him at his house in Pont Street. I made an appointment for a Saturday afternoon, my only free time, and went. It would have been a dream of a job: much of the time to travel with him on his yacht in the Mediterranean and the Persian Gulf, and help with his entertaining—French was essential for this, but there had been French quotations in my speech; when in London, to live in quarters of my own in the Pont Street house—bedroom, dining-room, sitting-room—and have meals there unless my attendance was required by my employer. He asked what I should want as salary?—I remember my reply: "I think what you want would be cheap at £250 a year." (This was a huge figure in those days.) He laughed and said he agreed. But alas, shorthand, both in English and in French, was a *sine qua non*, and I knew no shorthand; he was quite willing to wait for six months while I learned it, but I couldn't afford not to be earning for so long—we parted with mutual regret. I wish I could remember his name.

3

Cypher-breaking in the Admiralty
(DREAM)

1915

During the years from 1914 to 1918, war to people in England was such an unwonted state of affairs that the private impulse to do something to help was very strong. By 1915 most members of my family were actively working: both my brothers were at the front, Grace was a W.A.A.C. in France, Helen a civil servant in the Ministry of Munitions. But for a young married woman with a husband at home to look after—Owen was in the Foreign Office, so could not be released for active service—and a baby in arms, it was not so easy to find a job which could be undertaken alongside my personal commitments. I attended First Aid Classes, and went and did up clothing for refugees in Belgrave Square; but it all seemed rather futile, and when Joris Young rang up one day and asked if I would take on "a quite important job", in London, I was highly excited. I knew Joris slightly as Geoffrey Winthrop Young's eldest brother; with Geoffrey I had done a lot of climbing in Wales. On this occasion Joris was rather mysterious, and asked me to meet him next day at eleven o'clock by the south end of the bridge in St. James's Park; fizzing with curiosity, I went to keep the appointment.

But Joris was still mysterious. He began by asking how well I knew German? Pretty well, I told him; I had been brought up by German governesses, and spoke it constantly when we went to Switzerland in the summers—I could both read and write the Gothic script. He brushed the script aside, impatiently. Could I work from nine-thirty to six five days a week, and a half-day on Saturdays? Would I sign on for the whole war?—that was essential. I said that I should have to think it over. Well, could I let him know tomorrow? I promised to try. "You know Greta Robertson, don't you? You will be working with her," he said. "Goodbye," and he swung round abruptly and left me.

I went home thinking hard. Apart from the hours, the only hard fact that Joris had given me was that I should be working with Greta Robertson, whom I knew and greatly admired; before my poor Father's financial crash she had coached me in Italian history for a year or more. Of course Greta was bi-lingual in English and German, since her mother had been a niece of Bismarck; her brother was in the diplomatic service. Well, it would be nice to work with Greta, but signing on for the whole war!

The first thing was to find out what Patty felt about it. Patty was the baby's nurse; she had been mine when I was a child, and came back to me as soon as I had a baby of my own. If I was working all the week it would mean that Patty could only take her half-day on Saturdays or Sundays. This might not matter so much, since she was elderly and staid; moreover, she was a devout Methodist, and the most important feature of her week was her "meeting" on Sunday. But this would also mean that I could not easily go away for week-ends without defrauding the faithful soul of her free time.

I tackled her at once, so as to give her time to think it over before Owen came home in the evening. But Patty did not want to think it over at all. She was as patriotic as she was pious, and at once expressed the opinion that if there was something that I could do to help "the War", I ought to undertake it, "especially after all the money your Father spent on your education". Patty had always got on very well with my Father; his low-church views were the next best thing to Methodism. I broached the subject of week-ends—no, that did not matter; I should need to go and get a breath of air sometimes, and keep "the Master" company—the important thing was to win the war.

In the evening I put Joris's proposition up to Owen. Aunt Emily Graham was staying with us, and rather to my dismay she was considerably less enthusiastic than Patty; but Owen thought that on the whole I should at least try it on. He made light of my having to promise to work for the whole war—if I got ill I should just have to stop, but that was no reason why I shouldn't have a go. Then we speculated eagerly as to what this mysterious job could be. Joris had been in the Diplomatic Service, but had left it rather abruptly after a spell as Counsellor in Lisbon—we did not know what he was doing now, exactly; Owen thought he had heard that he had got some job in the Admiralty. Fluent German told us nothing; we were fighting the Germans, so perhaps translating documents, or some such thing? Anyhow, it was settled that I was to say Yes to Joris; I scribbled a note to that effect to take round to him first thing—he lived quite close by—and then, rather tired with so much excitement, I went to bed.

Now I had always been a great one for very vivid and detailed dreams; and what is more, I dream in colour, which according to Havelock Ellis only a small proportion of the human race does— it is more usual to dream in a sort of *grisaille*. Since my head was full of this unknown job when I went to sleep, it was not unnatural that I should dream about it—and I did.

This is what I dreamt. Joris met me somewhere in Whitehall, took me into a long narrow room with pale green walls, windows along one side, and several large tables on which lay foolscap-sized sheets of pale-green paper covered with horizontal lines of figures; Greta Robertson was there, and showed me what the work was: one put the sheets of paper into a machine rather like a cash-register, turned a handle, and the sheets came out with lines of typed words under the figures—the words were in German. So that was the job!—breaking German cyphers. What fun!

I got up early the next morning, ran round in bright sunshine to the little house where Joris and Helen, his wife, lived in Holland Street, and dropped my note into the letter-box. When I got back Owen and Aunt Emily were just starting breakfast—as I sat down I said, "Well, I know what the job is, anyhow. I'm going to bust German cyphers."

"Oh, Joris told you, did he?" Owen asked.

"No, I didn't see him; I put the note in the letter-box."

"Then how do you know?" Aunt Emily enquired rather sharply.

"I dreamt it."

"Mary Anne, how can you be so ridiculous?" she said, laughing; but Owen asked *what* I had dreamed—to him the idea of breaking cyphers did not appear so bizarre as it did to Aunt Emily. So I told them both my dream—I had two perfectly good witnesses, if only I could have used them!

Joris rang up later on and told me to be at the Admiralty at 11.15 and ask for him—when he came down he led me into the presence of a rather puffy old gentleman, Sir Alfred Ewing, the Director of Naval Education—such was the official umbrella under which Joris's little team was to be sheltered from prying eyes. Sir Alfred asked me a few questions, and then, without more ado, explained the nature of the work—Mr. Young was collecting a rather specialised group of people to break German cyphers—those which, so far, had defeated the efforts of the experts in Room 47. These other cyphers took too long, and Room 47 had to work fast. He then laid it on me that I must not tell *anyone* what I was doing, in any circumstances. I asked if I might not tell my husband?

"Certainly *not*," he said, with great emphasis. (Later I learnt the reason for this curious anxiety to keep the fact of Joris's activities from the Foreign Office; at the time I meekly gave my promise, inwardly lamenting the loss of my little triumph over my veridical dream.)

Just how truth-telling that dream was I soon learned. Joris now took me out again into Whitehall, crossed the road, and led me through a door between two shops—one was an A.B.C. We went up in a lift, and crossed a landing and an inner room; then he opened a door and stood aside for me to pass through. I stepped into a long narrow room with windows down one side, pale-green walls, and several tables, from one of which Greta Robertson rose to welcome me. Joris left us together, and Greta showed me piles of rather flimsy pale-green paper covered with lines of pencilled figures; these, she explained, were wireless intercepts, and our task was to learn to translate the figures into words. The only missing thing was the machine which in my dream had done the job for us—I looked round for it expectantly, but in vain. We were supplied with equipment for the purpose, but it was considerably more complicated to operate than turning the handle of a cash-register. On the table where I was to sit lay a foolscap-sized book bound in nubbly green material; most of the pages were blank except for a row of figures down the left-hand side, running from 1 to 10,000. This was to be the dictionary; our work was somehow to find out the meaning of the figures—they were mostly in groups of four—and then fill in the blank pages, till we could use the book *as* a vocabulary, and translate the telegrams as they came in.

This seemed to me tremendous fun, just the sort of job I should enjoy; I longed to start at once. But I had to go home and give Aunt Emily lunch; so promising to be there at 9.30 the following morning, I hurried away.

Of course Aunt Emily wanted to know what my work had turned out to be? I told her, with deliberate gloom, that I was to work for the Director of Naval Education, and that it was fearfully dull—a routine job, only involving some knowledge of German. Aunt Emily was delighted: she had an instinctive hostility to any ideas, or even facts, outside her personal ken, and truth-telling dreams certainly came into this category. The moment Owen came in that evening "It's all rubbish about Mary Anne's dream" she told him triumphantly. "She's only going to do a sort of clerk's work, but in German." Owen was less satisfied, and questioned me rather closely about my job; I did the best I could, but he didn't really believe me, I could see. However, there it was; my two perfectly good witnesses to my dream had to be sacrificed to "Security"—though I don't ever remember hearing that word in those days.

Next morning I went to the kitchen before breakfast and ordered the meals, and then to the nursery to see Patty and the baby, and tied a knot in my handkerchief to remind me to get Syrup of Figs in my lunch-hour; then I hurried to Earls Court Station and took the tube to Piccadilly—our "office" was almost at the top of Whitehall, near Trafalgar Square, so it was only a short run to it. That was the first day of a new routine that was to last for a long time.

The decyphering was fascinating. Everything one had ever heard or recalled about Germany seemed sooner or later to come in useful—old memories, current news, inspired guesses. As to the inspired guesses, I am sure that some para-normal faculty came into play. At one point someone said that the indelible-pencil figures on the green sheets of the wireless intercepts were trying to the eyes, and one of the girls was set to make typed copies of them. I *hated* these; I could not seem to get on with them at all—it was as though a fine film, or veil, was interposed between me and the meaning. In fact I believed then, and still believe, that the action of yet another human being on the figures, over and above the voice that spoke them into the ether, and the ear that heard and wrote them down, *did* do something to impede comprehension. This may sound, and be, silly; but it certainly operated in my case, quite apart from introducing a further factor of error.

4

Everest
(DREAM)

1924

In 1924 George Mallory set out with the third expedition to attempt to reach the summit of Mount Everest. My brother Jack and I had first met George at Zermatt in 1909, and both made friends with him; in fact he was the first friend I ever made independently and for myself, and so fell into a different category from the friends and acquaintances provided, so to speak, ready-made by my family—the children of my parents' friends, my sisters' dancing-partners. Till my marriage in 1913 George and I climbed a good deal together in Wales; we met in the Alps; he often stayed with us in London. In the summer of 1914 he married Ruth Turner, a niece of close friends of mine, Dr. and Mrs. Wills; soon the friendship with Ruth was as close as that with George himself. In 1917, when George was in France as a gunner, he and Ruth lent us The Holt, their house at Godalming; she was living with her family at Westbrook, just across the river, and we, with a young child, had decided to live out of London while the Zeppelins were menacing. Patrick, our son, was born at The Holt in 1918; it was Ruth who helped the local doctor to bring him into the world, because the monthly nurse had not arrived.

Naturally I took a great interest in the Everest expeditions. With George I pored over the routes and studied the photographs; when he was first asked to lecture about it I went and stayed with them, and George tried out his original lecture on Ruth and me, in his roomy study at The Holt—he was rather nervous, but in fact the lectures were a great success, delivered in his beautiful voice, with an engaging hint of shyness. Both Ruth and I noticed, though, before he left for the third time, that some of the happy enthusiasm that had been so evident before the two earlier expeditions was lacking—he was what he himself called "heavy", a frame of mind he detested if it took him before or during a climb.

We read of course in the papers every scrap of news that came from the expedition—always with a time-lag of about a fortnight while despatches were being brought down through Tibet by runners to the nearest telegraph office. Ruth was now living in Cambridge; they had settled there the winter before when George had taken a post as a University Extension Lecturer.

One night at the end of the first week in that June, at Bridge End, our house in Surrey, I had a peculiarly vivid dream. In it Ruth and I decided to go out and visit the Everest expedition. With the absurd inconsequence so frequent in dreams we took the train to Chur, in eastern Switzerland, and then drove in an open two-horse carriage through streets of high grey stone-built houses, till we reached the headquarters of the expedition. We went in; the men were all out, and we decided to get tea ready for them; there was no milk, so we took a large jug to the *Meierei*, the dairy along the street, and filled it—I clearly remember explaining the word *Meierei* to Ruth, who knew no German. Then the men came in, hungry and cheerful, with snowy boots, and we all had tea. And afterwards George took me into what he called the map-room, where there was a huge enlargement of a photograph of the ridge of Everest, running down to the North Col, on the wall; he took a thing like a billiard-cue and showed me the new camps, and explained how certain it was that they would reach the summit tomorrow. Then he put down the cue, and we sat on the big table in the middle of the room, swinging our legs, and talked— George spoke, more fully and openly than he had ever done before, to me, of what mountains and his relationship to mountains meant to him—he spoke with a strange mixture of reverence and what I can only call rapture.

This dream frightened me terribly. He had been so alive, so near, in it—just as when a beloved friend whom one has not seen for some time comes to stay, and for days after they have left the whole house is glowing and warm from their recent presence—so Bridge End, next morning, as I went about my daily tasks, was full of the presence of George. I did not want to worry Ruth, but I wrote to Marjorie Turner, her sister, at Westbrook, saying I had been worried by a dream, and asking what the latest news was of George? (I also asked her, urgently, to keep my letter and the envelope, with the post-mark—she didn't.) In reply I got a laconic post-card: "Last heard from R. three days ago; he was all right then. M."

I don't think I even tried to comfort myself with the absurd setting of the dream, like the Everest Expedition's headquarters being in a stone-built house in a Swiss town—I was too accustomed to the inconsequent dottiness of dreams. And on a Saturday morning nearly a fortnight later Owen came out to me where I was sorting linen in the big workroom behind the kitchen with the newspaper in his hand. "I've got some bad news for you," he said. "George and Irvine have been killed on Everest."

Odell reported having his last sight of the pair after noon on 8 June, above the last step, on the open snow arête, "going strongly for the top". Having climbed a lot with George, I cannot believe, with only a perfectly straightforward snow ridge between him and the summit, the last obstacle surmounted, that he did not reach it. And when in 1933 a later expedition found an ice-axe *below* the first rock step, it confirmed my belief, and that of many others, that Mallory and Irvine had reached the top, and that disaster had overtaken them on the way down. Descent is always more difficult than ascent; and who would leave an ice-axe behind, with that snow arête still in front of him? Certainly not George.

In 1953 Everest was successfully climbed by Hunt's party. I was in Ireland, but our daughter Jane, George's godchild, who was in London, telephoned me the news first thing. I was especially glad to hear it from her.

5

The Country Week-end
(KNOWING)

Denton 1925

In the early summer of 1925 I was staying with my father- and mother-in-law, Sir Edward and Lady O'Malley, at Denton, their old house outside Oxford. Owen, my husband, who was working in London at the Foreign Office, was coming down for the week-end, but on Thursday he telegraphed—there was no telephone then at Denton—to say that there was so much work that he should not, after all, come down till later on. I was disappointed, but not surprised; earlier in the year he had made a long official trip through Russia, Persia, Armenia and Turkey, and now, after such a long absence, he was very much by way of keeping his nose to the grindstone.

On the Saturday evening Aunt Winnie, as we called my mother-in-law, and I went up to bed at about half-past ten, carrying our candles in silver candlesticks; there was no electric light in the house, and as she went she put out the oil lamps in the hall and on the stairs. (She did not—rightly—trust old Sir Edward to do this safely; he had to go all the way by candle-light.) Usually there were only candles in the bedrooms at Denton, but as a special concession I was allowed a lamp, so that I could read in bed; it had already been lit and turned low, so that when I had kissed the old lady goodnight at my door, I had only to turn the lamp up, slowly and carefully, and soon the room was lit with that beautiful soft warm glow, so kind and gentle to the eyes—the kindest light there is. I drew the heavy red velvet curtains to keep out the moths, and washed in rather luke-warm water at the marble-topped wash-stand; there was no bathroom then at Denton, maids brought a hip-bath and cans of water to each bedroom in the morning. I undressed, and then knelt down to say my prayers—Aunt Winnie always went to Church, up on the hill at Cuddesdon, at 8 a.m., and on Sundays, when I was staying in the house, I went with her.

I was kneeling, then, at the side of the high, old-fashioned bed; my little red prayer-book, that I used in preparation for Holy Communion, lay on the faded quilt in front of me—I had closed it, and was saying my prayers, my face in my hands, when there came over me, quite suddenly, an overwhelming certainty that Owen was, at that moment, in acute temptation—physical temptation. I did not know with whom, nor where, except that it was in the country, I thought; but of its reality, and the desperate nature of the temptation, I had no doubt whatever. And abandoning my own prayers I prayed, with all my strength, that he should not "do anything that would make him unhappy afterwards". It is odd that that rather childish formula should remain so clearly in my mind; but that is what I prayed for, for some time. Then, feeling calmer, I finished my own prayers, and got into bed and went to sleep.

I can give no very good account of how this knowledge came to me. I saw nothing. I heard no words—although I remember so clearly the sense of my own prayer. But I never doubted for a moment that what I "knew", so strangely, was really taking place. And I was not mistaken. When, some days later, Owen came down to Denton he said as soon as we were alone—"There's something I want to tell you."

"I know," I said. "You went to the country last Saturday night."

He looked at me in astonishment. "Did —— write to you?"

"No"—and I told him exactly what had happened. He then

told me how he had got off from the Foreign Office that Saturday about six, too late to get to Oxfordshire; how he had met ——, a close friend of both of us, and how they had driven down to supper in Surrey and, the night being so lovely, had decided to take rugs and go up and camp out on the Downs—where, indeed, temptation had been strongly placed in his way, and had been resisted.

Years later the woman herself, with great generosity, volunteered an account of the episode to me—I felt almost ashamed that that unsought knowledge had come to me, and spoilt her idyll. She is now dead.

6

West Runton
(KNOWING)

1928

In the summer of 1928 my husband and I spent some weeks in the West Highlands, driving about in his car, seeing old friends and meeting new people. Presently he had to go South again and take up the fascinating job of helping Winston Churchill with his researches for *The Aftermath*, the fifth volume of his History of World War I; I stayed on in Scotland alone, to do some archaeology.

I had been engaged for some time in trying to make a complete *corpus* (comprehensive list) of all the West Highland tomb-slabs and crosses which bear the characteristic interlaced ornament; I had already found, and made rubbings on linen, of some 300 of them. What is still one of the best books on the subject in existence had been written many many years before by Owen's Uncle, Robert Graham of Skipness—*The Carved Stones of Islay*, with superb illustrations. Uncle Robert, with limitless time (and money), produced these by a very complicated process. The stone having been carefully cleared of soil and moss, so that the incised pattern was perfectly clear, sheets of "Barcelona paper", a thin but very tough fibrous brown paper, were moistened and gently beaten on to the surface with brushes; when fourteen layers had been beaten on and left to dry, they formed a mould strong enough to take a plaster cast; this was then made, propped upright, and photographed—the result was a flawless record of the complicated patterns. With a team of helpers, a van for all his plant, and a tent to erect over the stones while first the moulds and then the casts dried in the rainy climate of West Scotland, he spent happy weeks making these wonderful records.

Besides most of the stones on the island of Islay, he made a similar series on Mull; but he died before publishing these, and after his death in 1909 the set of superb negatives, thirty or more, was presented by his widow, Aunt Emily Graham, to the Museum of Antiquities in Edinburgh. But alas, if there ever had been a record of *where* on the island of Mull each stone was, it had not been preserved; and without this essential knowledge, the magnificent plates had lost much of their value, from the Museum's point of view. Now my much humbler rubbings had also been deposited in the Museum; on our way up to the West Highlands I had, as usual, dropped in to see the Curator, Dr. Callander, and hearing that I was going to the West again, he asked if I could not try to locate Uncle Robert's stones? He had a set of prints made, and posted them on to me in Lochaber—when Owen went South again, I made my way to Mull. My kit was much simpler than Uncle Robert's: a rucksack with a change of clothes and, more to the purpose, a 1-inch map of Mull, a trowel, a stout clasp-knife, several scrubbing-brushes, a note-book and half a dozen pencils and, most important of all, three sections of a cheap collapsible fishing-rod, to one of which was lashed a carving-knife.

Thus equipped, I tramped the roads of Mull, visiting the various graveyards marked on the map. The most likely for my purpose were the disused ones, overgrown with grass and bracken; once inside the crumbling stone walls I would first walk round and examine all stones lying on the surface—if none of these corresponded to any of the photographs Callander had given me, there began the rather laborious job, after putting the fishing-rod together, of prodding the turf with the carving-knife. This sometimes revealed the outline of a stone slab, but since they are practically all six or seven feet long even the prodding took some time; then, having stuck in twigs to mark the two ends, came the even more arduous task of cutting through the turf with my clasp-knife, and lifting the sods out with the trowel—it was nearly thirty years since Uncle Robert made his expedition to Mull, and some of the stones were under four or five inches of soil. Even when the sods were cleared away, the surface of the stone had to be thoroughly brushed to reveal the design—however, by these long and slow processes I identified several of those recorded in his photographs, as well as the relatively easy ones which were on the surface. Each stone was measured and described, and its situation in the graveyard noted—I had a prismatic compass, so that my bearings could be reasonably accurate; Dr. Callander had numbered the photographs, so that the situation of those I located was now made certain.

I did not find them all on that trip; I could only spare just over a fortnight, because I was due at home—Nannie had been alone with the two younger children long enough, and when Owen went to live with the Churchills at Chertwell, I felt I must go back. I had not been able to leave any firm address: there were next to no hotels in Mull in those days except at Tobermory, which was useless for my purpose, and I stayed where I could get a bed—sometimes at a farm, more often the local laird, whose permission I was always most careful to ask before I started "howking" on his land, put me up for two or three nights. But at one point I sent Nannie a telegram asking her to write to me Poste Restante, Oban, to say how they all were—I collected her letter some hours before I took my train South. It was completely reassuring—the children were all perfectly well, she said.

I assumed of course that this included Jane, who had gone to school for the first time just after Easter—to West Runton, near Cromer in Norfolk, whence she had written cheerfully if caustically during the first weeks of term; we had had letters from her

c

in Lochaber too, sent on by Nannie. When I got into the train at Oban I was not in the least worried about Jane.

I travelled third—we couldn't possibly afford sleepers, or even to travel first-class to or from Scotland at that stage of our married life, let alone to eat in the restaurant car; I bought some buttered scones and a lump of cheese and a couple of tomatoes, and made my frugal supper off those. As was often the case in the twenties, there was a map of the route the train took on the wall of the carriage; I looked at it idly, as one does, and noticed that we went through Peterborough, and that from Peterborough a small line meandered through King's Lynn and Fakenham to Cromer. Even then I didn't pay much attention; I smoked a cigarette after my supper and then, as I was alone in the carriage I wrapped myself in my burberry and using my rucksack as a pillow, lay down and went to sleep.

I am quite positive that on this occasion there was no question of my dreaming about Jane. It was quite different from that—something much more subtle and peculiar. At some point during the night, when the ticket-collector came in, I asked him if the train stopped at Peterborough—it did, soon after 7 a.m. I am not sure that even then I made up my mind to get out and go to West Runton, but by the morning my mind had made itself up. At Peterborough I got out, took that slow train that crawled through the rather flat country south of the Wash, stopping at practically every station till it reached West Runton; here I again got out, put my luggage in the cloakroom, and walked along to the school.

Of course I asked for the head-mistress, but I don't think she was there—certainly it was a rather junior and very embarrassed matron who eventually greeted me with the words "Oh, I *am* thankful that you have come!" She took me to the sick-bay, where Jane lay in bed, protesting that she felt perfectly well, "or nearly perfectly", except for a slight pain in her side; she had, however, a persistent temperature, which completely defeated the local doctor. Somehow we got hold of one who had the wits to have tests made; she had tuberculosis of the kidney. Owen came up with the car, and we took her down to London, where she was put in a nursing-home, first for a cystoscopy—mercifully only one kidney was affected, which was removed in a second operation a week later. Speed was of the essence; if the second kidney had become infected nothing could have saved her. She hated the nursing-home (I think not without some reason) and lay in bed chanting, loudly, her own parody of the children's hymn "Jesus loves me".

> "Sister loves me, she who brings
> All those nasty pills and things
> Tells me that my food's so nice
> When it's only cold boiled rice.
> Yes, Sister loves me,
> Yes, Sister loves me,
> Yes, Sister loves me
> The Doctor tells me so."

When she was well enough to travel we went out to Chateau d'Oex for six months; she made a complete recovery, but it was a very close call, the doctors all said.

Why did I get out of the train at Peterborough?

7

Abbotsford
(DREAM)

1935 or '36

In the late autumn of 1935 or 1936 I was asked to go and give a lecture in Edinburgh by some literary society or other; by this time my books had begun to appear, and I was often asked to lecture. The chairman on this occasion was to be Lady Maxwell-Scott, wife of Sir Walter Maxwell-Scott of Abbotsford, and soon after I had agreed I got a letter from her, inviting me to go up the day before and stay for the lecture, and the following week-end. I did not remember having met Lady Maxwell-Scott, though she averred that we had done so in London, but I gladly accepted. In a later letter confirming the arrangements she said that the car and chauffeur would meet my train at Galashiels and take me out to the house—the night train from London arrived at the godless hour of 6 a.m. or thereabouts, and she hoped I would go to bed and "finish the night", and she would see me later in the morning. This all seemed very kind and sensible, and when the due date arrived I went up from the country to London and set off from King's Cross.

Thanks to the success of my books to take a sleeper to Scotland was no longer an impossibility; I settled down comfortably in mine, got out my despatch-case, and put a few finishing touches to my lecture, so as to be perfectly ready for the following evening, and then went to sleep. I was called by the attendant in good time, and was all ready to get out when the train drew up, in the pitch darkness of six o'clock of a November morning, at the station.

Sure enough, a car was waiting, and I was whisked off along dark roads towards my destination—in fact I fell asleep again, and was only aroused when the car stopped at a lighted hall door. A sleepy footman took my luggage and led me upstairs, where an equally sleepy housemaid unpacked while I had a bath, and then brought me breakfast in bed. Nothing could have been more comfortable or more pleasant—there was a blazing fire, I lay in a luxurious bed and ate my breakfast; when the maid came to take away the tray I asked to be called at eleven, and then went to sleep again.

I suppose anyone might have been expected to experience a certain degree of interest in finding themselves actually staying in the house which the great Sir Walter Scott built for himself, where he passed his later years, and eventually died. I am afraid I did not. Perhaps I was given the Waverley Novels to read at the wrong age—indeed not only given them, but forced to read some, such as Kenilworth and Ivanhoe; anyhow I found them unendurable: long-winded, boring, and somehow bogus (though that word was not in use then, I fancy.) And I transferred my dislike of the books to the innocent author. I really knew nothing about him; I had never bothered to read Lockhart's Life, and indignantly rejected the praise lavished on him in the manuals of English literature dutifully given us by our German governesses. Which makes what follows all the more curious.

During that morning sleep at Abbotsford I had a long and very detailed dream. I dreamt, first, that I was in the room where I had in fact just fallen asleep by firelight, and that I was roused by my hostess coming in to see me while I was still in bed; in the dream she was tall, thin, and very Scottish-looking (completely unlike the reality which I was shortly to encounter). She left me after a few minutes, saying that lunch would be at 1.30; I got up and dressed and proceeded downstairs, intending to go out into the garden. At the foot of the stairs was a large hall, at one side of which a door stood open; as I stepped into the hall a little dog ran out through this door, barking sharply—startled, I gave a little scream, and a man's voice called through the door, rather irritably —"Who is *that*?" I went over and entered the room, saying "It's Mrs. O'Malley—the dog startled me." A tall, thin, grey-haired man rose from behind a laden desk, and introduced himself as my host; beside him stood a shorter and stouter man, in a suit of tweed of a peculiar dark brownish red, already familiar to me as crotal (a natural dye made from lichen)—he was introduced to me as the factor, as the Scots call a land-agent.

We exchanged a few words, and then, still in the dream, I went out through the front door, and found myself in a large walled space from which a drive led off on one side. The high stone walls which partly surrounded it were covered almost to the top with a thick growth of some green shrub or creeper; at intervals this had been cut away in ovals to reveal stone carvings, a most peculiar feature. From here I made my way out into the garden, and wandered about; shaven lawns sloped down to a river.

Returning to the house by a different route, I noticed an open french window, and went in; inside I found my Scottish-looking hostess, accompanied by two little girls, dressing a Christmas-tree—I stood and watched them. A yard or two away from me was a high, very slender ebony table on three legs, whose round top was only some nine inches across; on it stood a tall white china vase decorated with forget-me-nots, whose blue petals and gold stamens were embossed on the white glaze—a pretty, delicate thing. We began talking about the Christmas-tree, when suddenly I noticed that, though I had not moved, the slender black table with its brittle ornament was standing close by my elbow. I moved away a couple of yards, and went on chatting; but in a moment or two, there was the black table with the forget-me-not vase at my side again, almost as if it were nudging me. This happened several more times, and at last in desperation I said to my hostess—"Lady Maxwell-Scott, I'm worried about this

table; I'm afraid of the vase getting broken—but whatever I do, it seems to follow me about."

"Oh," she replied, quite unconcerned, "it always does that to those who love the house, and whom the house loves."

Soon after this surprising reply I left the room, and presently went out of the house again on the farther side. Here I found myself on a stone path which seemed to follow the top of the wall bounding the garden; it was some ten feet above the lawns, studded with large trees, which lay below on my left; to my right open country stretched away. I could not see this very well, as there was a grassy bank above the path on that side; presently, as I walked along, I came on some workmen sitting on this bank in the sun, eating their lunch. And just then I noticed a curious thing: the whole path, bank and workmen and all, seemed to be moving forward with a slow steady motion, as an escalator moves upwards on the Underground. I paused, and asked one of the workmen how this came about? He replied, in a deep voice—"There's them below that has plenty of strength to carry it."

This reply, delivered in deep, solemn tones, startled me so much that I woke up. I was in my room; the fire had burnt low; my watch showed that it was nearly eleven. I got up, drew back the curtains, and began to dress; after a few minutes the maid came in, bringing fresh coffee—she made up the fire, and told me that lunch would be at 1.30. No hostess came near me. When I had finished dressing and drunk a cup of coffee, I put on a jacket and set out to explore.

A curious feature of Abbotsford is that the passages are lit almost entirely by skylights; the great Sir Walter, who designed the house himself, was determined that none of the lovely views should be wasted on people hurrying along corridors, so every room has a view, and the passages only skylights. After some false shots I managed to find a staircase, and went down it; I had almost reached the hall at the bottom when from an open door on my right a little dog rushed out, barking. I gave a tiny scream, and from the open door a man's voice said irritably, almost angrily—"Who is *that*?" Just as in my dream, I went across and through the open door; just as in my dream, a tall grey-haired man, Sir Walter Maxwell-Scott, stood up behind his desk and introduced himself. I looked eagerly to see if the man in the crotal tweed suit was there too—yes, sure enough, he was, and was duly presented as the factor. (I think his name was Curle.) We talked for a little while, and then I went back into the hall and out through the front door; there was that very peculiar walled space, with the ovals of carving set in the solid thickness of the greenery, just as I had dreamt it barely an hour before.

But there the correspondence of dream with reality stopped. When I went on to take my stroll in the garden there was no open french window, no moving wall; and when I finally encountered my hostess she was not the tall angular Scotswoman of my dream, but a neat petite dark-haired lady who looked, as indeed she was, completely French. That evening we drove into Edinburgh—where she took the chair most efficiently at my lecture—and drove out again. And then, for the next three days, under my host's guidance, I was shown Abbotsford thoroughly—and to be shown Abbotsford thoroughly is, practically, to meet Sir Walter Scott.

This dream of mine must seem, though certainly peculiar, utterly pointless—if it has any point it lies, precisely, in the life and character of the author of the Waverley Novels. Much as I had detested these, and in consequence their author, I could not go on disliking poor old Sir Walter when I had seen the very desk and chair at which he had sat, day after day, month after month, year after year—writing, writing, writing to make money enough to pay off the vast debts which he had incurred over building the house of his dreams; still less after taking my meals for several days in the dining-room into which, at the last, he had had his bed wheeled, so that his dying eyes might rest on the view he loved most of all—the view that caused him to build Abbotsford exactly there. One could not but be touched by the eager enthusiasm which caused him to instal the first private gas-plant in Britain, to light Abbotsford by gas; two of the old retorts used to stand flanking the front door—perhaps they still do.

And the books! Sir Walter's Library was vast; four men, who in summer showed tourists over the house and grounds, were now fully employed during the winter months in looking after this— dusting the books, and polishing the covers with neatsfoot oil, to nourish the leather and keep it in good condition; I saw them doing it. One section, kept behind locked doors of wire mesh, was devoted entirely to magic and the black arts—my host told me that this section alone contained 13,000 volumes. Thirteen thousand books on magic! I felt this went some way to explain why, asleep under that roof, I should have dreamed such a strange dream of the moving wall and the affectionate table—for in the end I did become one of those who loved the house, monstrous as it is.

What interests me particularly about this dream is the curious mixture of truth and fantasy, of accuracy and inaccuracy. Why should the twentieth-century Sir Walter Maxwell-Scott and his factor have presented themselves to me in advance exactly as they were, down to their very clothes and words, whereas Lady Maxwell-Scott came out entirely wrong? Why should the dream have shown me that very peculiar enclosed forecourt (in fact it now has a garden in part of it), so correctly, and invented the non-existent wall with a path along the top? In fact, as I have said, I think the great Sir Walter's obsession with magic, lingering in the house along with the thirteen thousand volumes, may somehow have produced the fantastic part of the dream, but why should this have been combined with something that was much more like a slip in time, as in the episode of the Ascot procession? But in

Windsor Great Park I was broad awake, holding my pony carefully so that it should not stumble on that rough steep track.

That an emotion or preoccupation can leave a strong effect hanging about an actual place is shown very clearly in the next episode.

8

Blois
(NIGHTMARE)
1937

In the autumn of 1937 my husband was sent as British Minister to Mexico. Our youngest daughter had two more terms to finish out at school, and there were no very suitable relations with whom she could be sent to spend her holidays; on the other hand our eldest girl had just come down from Oxford. So it seemed a good plan that she should go out with her Father and spend the next eight months being mistress of a Legation, learning things quite different to what tutors teach in Modern Greats, while I stayed at home to look after Kate.

However during term-time there was not much looking after to be done, so when a young engaged couple said how nice it would be if I would chaperone them on a tour by car of the Loire *chateaux*, I gladly agreed—I had never seen Amboise or Chambord or any of those places, and had always wanted to. However, I insisted on beginning with Rouen, and then taking in Evreux and Chartres; so we had been some days on the road when, as the autumn dusk was falling, we drove into Blois, which we had decided to make our centre for the Loire country.

In those days the Guide Bleu only featured two really good hotels in Blois, the *Hôtel de France et de Guise* and the *Hôtel Blois*— we opted for the *France*. However, we followed our usual prudent practice of parking the car and leaving one of the party in charge of it, while the others went on foot to the hotel and booked rooms; to drive up in an at all respectable car to the door of a

French hotel put a considerable percentage on to the price of rooms, and my Talbot coupé was rather more than respectable. Even so the rooms were not really cheap at the *France*; by mid-October the central heating was already necessary, but for economy it was only put on as high as the first floor, so we had perforce to take first-floor rooms. We bargained a bit, and eventually I was given a big double room with a bathroom, while the young people had two small singles close by. Then we went and fetched the car and the luggage—great was the *patron*'s chagrin when he saw the Talbot, but the price had been fixed, and that was that. By the time we had settled in, and established that the place was nice and clean and the water hot, it was fairly late; we went down and had a perfectly tolerable dinner, and then went straight to bed—we had had a long day. But we were all in the best of spirits—here we were at Blois, in the heart of the Chateaux country, in golden autumn weather, all set to enjoy ourselves.

I am normally, and have been for most of my life, a particularly good sleeper, even if only stretched out on the seat of a third-class carriage with a knapsack for a pillow, as on my return from Scotland in 1928. There is a technique about sleeping, I believe; an attitude of mind which enables one to ignore noise, as well as the conscious relaxing of the muscles. But there was no obvious need for any techniques that night in the *France*—the bed was perfectly comfortable, I was healthily tired, and looking forward with pleasure to the day ahead; I fell asleep at once.

I woke, perspiring and terrified, out of a horrifying nightmare; the details have become vague, but the predominant emotion was of an impulse to commit suicide—my watch showed that I had only been asleep about an hour. Irritated, for I value my night's rest, I took an aspirin and settled down again. As before, I fell asleep quickly, but was frightened wide awake by another, similar nightmare, again suicidal in content; and again I had barely been asleep an hour. This time I took some trouble about calming down—I lit a cigarette, took two aspirins, and read a book for half an hour before putting out the light and lying down. Going to sleep was again no trouble, but as on both the earlier occasions, another suicidal nightmare ensued—they went on all night. When the young people came in the morning to take their baths in my bathroom and to consume their *petits déjeuners* in my spacious bedroom, I told them firmly that I didn't like the hotel, and that we must move that very morning, to the *Hôtel Blois*. They grumbled a little—they had hoped to spend the morning exploring the town; but I was adamant, and by twelve noon (the hour by which one must have vacated one's room in a hotel in France if one is not to pay for another twenty-four hours) we had packed, paid our bill, and transferred to the other hotel. Three people and their luggage leaving one hotel and going to another, just because of some bad dreams—doesn't it seem absurd? But that is what happened.

We spent a very happy ten days in Blois. The Loire country in October is enchanting, with high bright skies and clear sunshine —long lines of poplars stretching across the arable, pale stubble and gleaming brown newly-ploughed land; as the leaves came off the poplars we saw that the whole country is full of mistletoe, hanging in green bunches, like huge birds nests, dark against the pale sky—indeed we learned that it is an article of export. We examined the chateaux thoroughly—Amboise, with its extravagant nonsense of winding inclined planes up which a carriage and horses could be driven from the bottom of the building to the top; Chambord, enormous and much less elegant; Chaumont and Cheverny, and the beautiful town of Tours. (Here, in a very small street, we came on a tiny shop whose single little window, which contained a tennis-racquet and nothing else, bore the extravagant notice—"*Tout pour le tennis, le sporting, et le camping.*") We went as far afield as Chinon, to see the bare spare apartment, with unglazed slits for windows, in which Joan of Arc spent the night before her momentous meeting with the Dauphin—when we exclaimed at the draughtiness the rather lackadaisical youth who was showing us over remarked, through his cigarette—"*Dans les jours de Jeanne d'Arc, ceci c'etait le confort moderne!*" And in the chateau at Blois itself, of course, we came up against the elegantly flamboyant personality of Francis the First himself, with his so inappropriate symbol of the hedgehog, the *porc-épic*, carved everywhere—on mantelpieces, over doors and windows—wherever it could possibly be displayed.

The wealth of chateaux in Touraine becomes almost overwhelming, and on the very last day we were quite glad just to drive through the forests of Blois, and of Russy, and to look at some of the smaller and simpler things near at hand, like the delicious little Chateau du Moulin, its four corner towers reflected in its narrow moat. On our way back towards Blois my eye was caught by a sign-post with the name Cour-Cheverny, and I remembered that it was at Cour-Cheverny that Patrick, my son, had spent some months a year or two earlier learning French in a family presided over by an elderly Countess whom he called Tante Odette—I have now forgotten her surname, but I remembered it then, and decided to look her up. To Cour-Cheverny accordingly we went, and after enquiries found the Countess; she professed great pleasure at meeting Patrick's mother, and insisted on our staying to tea—the usual horrible French meal of very weak tea and rather dry and withered *petits-fours*.

But that visit produced some rather startling information. Tante Odette asked where we were staying in Blois? At the *Hôtel Blois*, I told her—"We spent the first night at the *France*, but we didn't like it, so we moved on to the other, where we have been perfectly comfortable."

The old lady suddenly displayed great animation.

"*Tiens!*—you stayed at the *France*! Did they show you *la chambre de Madame Simpsonne? Une grande belle chambre au première étage?—le numero neuf!*" She went on to explain that the chamber-maid for the first floor at the *Hôtel de France* came from the village of Cour-Cheverny, and she, Tante Odette, had learned from the woman all the dramatic doings when Mrs. Simpson, on her hurried departure from England at the time of the Abdication crisis, not quite a year before, had spent a night in Blois on her way down to the Riviera—the Press were so hard on her heels that early the next morning she was smuggled out before daybreak by the aperture through which coal was normally shovelled in, and taken several kilometres in a taxi to rejoin her car, at a point well out in the country.

But the *femme-de-chambre* had given still more illuminating details about that night. I repeat them in French, in the words which Tante Odette gave, so excitedly, to me that autumn afternoon in 1937.

"*Elle s'est couchée toute habillée!*" (She went to bed with all her clothes on.) "*Elle ne se sera pas beaucoup lavée, la pauvre, car les serviettes n'etaient pas même défaites!*" (She can't have done much washing, poor thing, for the face-towels weren't even unfolded.) I can hear the old Frenchwoman's staccato, emphatic tones now, as she brought out this piteous account of a woman in dire distress, at a crucial moment in her life.

The room at the *Hôtel de France* where I had those appalling nightmares, which caused us to pack up and leave the very next day, was Number 9—*la chambre de Madame Simpsonne*. I personally have no doubt but that at some point that night she contemplated suicide. I am glad she decided against it; I venture to think that she has made a very good wife to not the happiest of men. Neither of the hotels at which we stayed appears in the most recent edition (1958) of the Guide Bleu that I have been able to lay my hand on; Blois was badly knocked about in 1940, during the war, and much of the town has been rebuilt since then. If that particular room no longer exists, I personally think it is just as well.

Note. Since writing this I have managed to get hold of the Duchess of Windsor's autobiography, *The Heart has its Reasons.* She does not mention the coal-shoot; this may have been a flight of imagination on the part of the chamber-maid from Cour-Cheverny. Or it may not. The book is highly selective, as personal recollections tend to be. (Having written two volumes of these myself, I recognise selectivity when I see it; and we were at the Legation in Peking when the Duchess, as Mrs. Spencer, was there in the twenties—the selectivity in that section is extreme.) But she does mention the sense of desperation (she uses the word) as a "relentless companion" on that whole journey to the South of France.

PART II

Two first-hand accounts
of Individual Experiences

Accounts received at first hand

So far I have confined myself to my own immediate personal experiences of extra-sensory perception, in dreams and waking "knowings". I will now give an account of two which were told to me direct by a person to whom they happened—in the first case my mother, in the second my father-in-law, the late Sir Edward O'Malley.

My mother was an American, the youngest of a family of five sisters and two brothers; her people, the Days, came partly from New England, partly from the South; she herself was born, and for the most part brought up, in New Orleans, where she met, and married, my father. Her eldest brother James, to whom she was passionately devoted, as little sisters sometimes are, never married; he had a roving temperament, and presently wandered off to the expanding tracts in the West. At the time of his death I was a little girl myself, and I remember clearly what my mother, later, told me about it. While my father was away on one of his frequent business journeys overseas she had a sudden overwhelming certainty that her brother Jim was in some serious danger; so deep was her concern that she actually cabled to her parents to ask for news of him. Because of the cable, this "knowing" of hers was well documented, for she wrote down both the cost and the date in her account-book—my father was very rigid about accuracy in such matters. An answering cable came the next day—"No news of Jim for six weeks was well then." But a little later came first

another cable, and then a letter, telling of Uncle Jim's death out in
the far West, from some sudden illness; the letter gave the actual
date of his death. He had died on the very day on which my
mother sent her cable of enquiry, and wrote it down in her
account-book.

Old Sir Edward O'Malley's experience was supported by
equally good documentary evidence—in fact even better, since
in his case two people recorded the relevant date. And it is, to me,
a particularly interesting example, because in this case what I can
only call the "message" did not reach the person it was meant for,
but somebody else who was with him at the time, and in a garbled
form at that. It is rather a long story; I will tell it as briefly as
I can.

Sir Edward held various legal appointments under the old
Colonial Office, and spent much of his life, in perfect health and
great contentment, in parts of the world formerly described as
"white man's graves". On his retirement, before becoming Chairman of Quarter Sessions at Oxford, a post he held for some seventeen years, to occupy his unwanted leisure he interested himself in
various charities, one of which he always referred to simply as
"The Shoe-Blacks".

The Shoe-Blacks—I never knew their real style and title—con-
sisted mainly of a hostel run by a Warden and a Matron, where
small boys from "bad homes", or orphans, were placed, to be fed
and clothed and decently looked after. For a livelihood they were
fitted out with little red monkey-jackets and pill-box caps and
sent forth—equipped with brushes, blacking, kneeling-mats for
themselves and foot-rests for their clients' feet—to such favourable
spots as Charing Cross Station, Trafalgar Square, Piccadilly
Circus and so on. There the little creatures knelt and plied their
trade, calling "Shine your shoes, Sir?" to the passers-by. Their
very modest takings—"a shine" only cost a penny, or two-pence
if brown—did not nearly pay for their board and lodging, let

alone the wages of the Warden and Matron; the committee of gentlemen who organised the charity subscribed what was necessary for this. Today the whole thing would be utterly frowned upon; but the otherwise neglected children were cared for, they earned an honest living, and when they grew older it was, seemingly, fairly easy for the members of the Committee to place any former shoe-black in some decent occupation. Moreover the Committee helped to feed them off their own estates.

This last aspect led to my hearing, from Sir Edward's own lips, one of the most curious examples of supra-normal communication I have ever come across. At one point it was discovered that the Warden of the boys' hostel had taken to drink, and absented himself at night; he was summoned before the Committee, and given notice. His wife, the Matron, an excellent woman, then did a sort of importunate widow act, and vowed that if "the gentlemen" would give her husband another chance, she would see to it that he was never out at night again. After some discussion—in her absence—it was decided to give the man another trial; but the members of the Committee arranged between themselves that two of their number should occasionally pay surprise visits to establish whether the Warden really was staying in at night. One evening, accordingly, after dining at their club, Sir Edward and a Colonel Y—I have forgotten his name—visited the hostel together; to their great dismay, for everyone liked and respected the wife, the husband was out. The poor woman, sobbing, declared that he had only gone to see his sick mother, and implored them not to report him. They agreed together to say nothing until they had paid another visit—but both carefully noted the occurrence, with the date and time, in their diaries.

A few weeks later they went to the hostel again. This time the Warden was in; they were invited into the neat parlour, and shown some of the little shoe-blacks asleep in bed—all was serene. But as they were leaving the Matron said to Colonel Y—

"You never sent me those wild-duck, Sir, that you promised me the last time you came."

"Wild-duck?" said the Colonel, astonished.

"Yes, Sir. You said you'd been shooting wild-duck, and you promised to send me a hamperful for the boys, to make a change for them."

Now it was a regular custom for the members of the Committee who had shootings to send some of their game to the hostel —rabbits, hares, occasionally venison. But Colonel Y had no duck-shooting, and therefore was positive that he could not have promised the good woman a hamper to vary "the boys'" diet. He left completely puzzled (as was Sir Edward) promising to send some rabbits, of which he had plenty, as soon as he could.

Colonel Y received the explanation, for what it was worth, of the Matron's words a few days later, when the Admiralty wrote to inform him, with deep regret, of the death of his brother, a Commander in the Navy. The Commander had gone ashore in the Falkland Islands to shoot wild-duck; there had been an accident, and he had been killed by his own gun. The official letter gave the date and time of the accident; these corresponded correctly with the Colonel's and Sir Edward's first interview with the Matron at the hostel, when her husband had been out, as recorded in their diaries. Now Sir Edward had been present on this occasion, and heard all that passed: there had been no mention of wild-duck shooting, he told me, and no promise by the Colonel such as the Matron described. Here was the *psi* factor, or whatever it is called, in action; that the transmission should have missed the person who was presumably its mark, the Colonel, and as it were hit the Matron instead, makes it, to me, all the more convincing— it is like the bending of a ray of light passing through water. And the woman had naturally translated whatever strange message reached her into the terms of her own immediate preoccupation, namely providing as varied a diet as possible for her boys. A very curious story, and splendidly documented by the diaries of two such thoroughly senior and responsible people as an ex-Colonel and a Colonial Judge.

This business of *translation* into terms of the recipient's own manner of life and private preoccupations is, I am sure, very important; one feels one is up against that, sometimes, in the utterances of the Old Testament prophets—the divine message is there, but so wrapped up in a mode of life and thought completely different from our own as to lose much of its impact, for us. Reading the Old Testament one comes to feel, in a curious way, the much greater *limpidity* of certain of the prophets: Isaiah, for example, seems to transmit the divine idea in a purer form than do Ezekiel or Jeremiah.

The experiences so far recorded have all come entirely unsought —thrust, as it were, from without upon passive recipients. But mankind has long been aware of his supra-normal powers, and has used them, quite deliberately, for his own purposes. One of the commonest of these manifestations is, I suppose, dowsing—finding water or, more rarely, metals, underground by holding a forked twig in both hands; the twig, in the hands of a dowser, jerks violently when over water, or the object sought. (Oddly enough I am unable to do this myself; but I have felt the fierce motion of the twig when a dowser let me lay my hands over his —the wood *wrenches* at the controlling hands, like a live thing trying to escape.) Then there are various forms of requesting information—table-turning, automatic writing and so on, leading on to the whole business of psychic mediums and "controls". This last I have rather steered clear of; I can't disbelieve in it, but I just don't care for it. I have never wanted to consult a medium, and have never done so; having my hand read by a palmist, and my fortune told by gypsies, is as far as I have gone in that direction —never with any very spectacular results that I can recall!

But there is one rather simple and straightforward method of consulting powers beyond our normal ken which was much in vogue in my youth, in which I have often taken part—setting the whole alphabet, in large cardboard letters, out in a circle on a bare table, and placing a tumbler upside down in the middle; the participants (four is usually the maximum) each place a finger on the top of the reversed tumbler, and when a question has been addressed to it it starts moving about and touching the letters in turn, so spelling out a reply. I believe that this was the method used by Schumann's niece (or daughter?) to discover the where-abouts of his last concerto; certainly Jelly d'Aranyi used it success-fully to re-discover this same concerto in this century. Of course for this to work, all those taking part must be honest, and not give the tumbler a deliberate impetus towards any letter; but it is not usually impossible to find four honest people, who are patient enough and interested enough to give the thing a trial. (And in fact once the tumbler is really "working", it is almost impossible to control.) Sometimes nothing happens: when the tumbler is asked aloud—"Is anyone there?" it races with great decision to spell out "NO", jabbing at the two adjoining letters. If it says "YES", the usual procedure is to ask—"Have you got a message for anyone?" and then, "For whom?" This may be one of the players, or someone present in the room; less usually, the message is for someone who is not there. Occasionally some frivolous or mis-chievous entity seems to take charge, pouring out nonsense or even bad language; in that case we used to stop, and try again later. "Oh, it's you again, you stupid creature!" I have heard my husband exclaim disgustedly at Skipness, Aunt Emily Graham's house in Argyllshire, where we did a lot of tumbler-pushing, when the frivolous being kept on coming and controlling the glass. Nor do I ever remember our getting any very outstanding results there. But one rather remarkable message was passed to Ruth Mallory, after George Mallory's death, in her absence—I set that down as it was told to me by Will Arnold-Forster, the artist, who was present.

Will at this time was living at The Eagle's Nest, his house on the lip of the cliffs above Zennor in Cornwall. Some friends of his had taken a farmhouse up on the moors about a mile away; when they went abroad for a holiday they lent the farm to friends of theirs, whom he did not know, and asked him to be civil to them—so one evening, after a long day's painting, he walked up after supper to call on these strangers. He found them gathered round a table, bare except for a circle of letters and a glass, all set for a session of tumbler-pushing; they invited him to join them. Will took no interest in the *au delà*, in fact rather disliked the whole idea; he refused to touch the tumbler, but out of politeness let himself be persuaded to act as "recorder"—to sit with a pad and pencil and jot down in succession the letters indicated by the glass.

They got off to a brisk start. "Yes" proclaimed the glass at once, on being asked if anyone was there?—and "Yes" again, when asked if it had a message for anyone. Who for? "For Ruth." Will began to pay a little more attention—while the others were discussing who "Ruth" might be (they could not think of any Ruth they knew very well) he remembered Ruth Mallory, whom he then knew only slightly, widowed not long before. He asked his hosts to enquire who the message was from? "George" came back at once. "George who?" Will persisted—the answer was "George Mallory".

Now everyone was at once deeply interested. The tragedy of Everest was still fairly recent, and the idea of being in touch with Mallory himself was almost frightening; though it must be remembered that none of the people whose fingers were actually on the tumbler knew that his wife was called Ruth—Will, who did know this, never touched the glass at any point; he merely sat by the table, writing down the letters as they were touched. From this point onwards, though, he told me that he asked most of the questions—certainly it was he who asked what the message for Ruth was.

"Tell her she must do something about Frank," came the reply. Will was completely stumped by this. None of George's three children was called "Frank"; his only brother's name was

Trafford. Puzzled, uncertain, half-incredulous, but anxious to do the right thing by Ruth, if this really were a message from George, he asked what Ruth was to do about Frank?

"He's unhappy—she must do something about him," was all the reply he got. Utterly baffled, Will nevertheless wrote to Ruth Mallory—who had by this time returned to her family home at Godalming, Westbrook—and told her what had happened; rather apologetically, since the name "Frank" conveyed nothing to him; he was afraid of bothering her about what might prove to be a nonsense. On the other hand he dared not suppress what just conceivably might, he reluctantly admitted, be a genuine message from George.

The message was genuine enough. Just after the First World War some charitable organisation had evacuated a number of young children from Vienna, where practically famine conditions persisted, and placed them in families in England; one such child, called Franz, had been taken in at Westbrook, and remained there for three or four years. When conditions in Vienna improved his mother, a widow, asked to have him back, and he was duly sent home—but latterly news of him had become rather scanty. On getting Will's letter Ruth Mallory at once guessed that the "Frank" of the tumbler-pushers down in Cornwall might well be Franz, and somehow arranged for enquiries to be made on the spot in Vienna. In fact the child was in great need; his mother had re-married, he was neglected and very unhappy. Ruth and her sisters got him back to England again, and Westbrook once more became his home; from there he was sent first to school, then to college, and finally was launched as a craftsman in a trade for which he showed a marked aptitude; from Westbrook he eventually married, and is now successfully running his own business in England.

What I find so interesting about this episode is that the circumstances practically preclude any possibility of fraud or tampering on the part of those who had their hands on the glass. None of them knew Ruth Mallory, still less Frank or Franz. Will Arnold-Forster, the reluctant recorder, with a built-in distaste for the whole enterprise, had never heard of Franz's existence—and since none of the party were German-speakers they between them did their own bit of "translation" (like the Matron at the hostel), changing the name Franz to Frank.

To turn to the better-known and more practical matter of water-divining, commonly called "dowsing" by the country-people. The first time I actually saw this done was at Skipness; the practitioner was Owen's cousin, Frances Graham, who was very good at it—both she and the locals took her powers in this matter completely for granted, though surface-water in Argyllshire is so abundant that the underground supply seldom had to be sought. However, there were occasions—and I was the unexpected cause of one. During one visit, because there were a great many guests in the house, I was asked to use Aunt Emily's own bathroom; this had that peculiarly annoying form of plug, a vertical tube with holes in the bottom three inches, through which the water was supposed to escape while the tube was lodged on a special ring at the top. I was unfamiliar with this contraption, failed to find the ring, and pulled the tube right out. But alas, I had left my wash-rag and sponge—yes, we used large natural sponges in those days—in the bath, and to my dismay away they went down the drain. Not only was I left ragless and spongeless, but that drain, which served another bath as well as a housemaid's sink, soon showed itself to be blocked; neither of the baths, nor the sink, could be emptied. Aunt Emily was naturally very cross. I was crushed with shame.

Of course Frances was applied to, to locate the stoppage; from where that drain left the house it was 200 yards or more across the garden to its outflow on the shore. (Sewage from the house was of course treated quite separately.) Frances went to her room and fetched her forked hazel twig, and together we went down to the shore and found the outflow, now not flowing, only dripping feebly; we returned to the garden, which was surrounded by a high stone wall, but we had marked the drain's exit by a particular shrub, and inside the wall found its faint outline in the grass. Holding the twig in front of her in both hands, Frances moved towards the house—here and there she was impeded by a bed of shrubs or flowers, but she held to the general line till, about fifty yards from the house, on a smooth stretch of lawn, the twig began to jerk violently in her hands. While I waited at the spot she went on up to the house, the twig jerking all the way; then she came back to where I stood, and at once the twig's movement ceased. Alan, one of the gardeners, was sent for, and dug down two or three feet till he came to the drain-pipes; there was a joint just there, and a piece of pipe had to be broken; my sponge had stuck at the join. Alan had to wait till all the water penned up in the pipe had run off, and he could remake the join with mortar; Aunt Emily was still cross, but Bertie Graham, who ran the place since Uncle Robert's death, only laughed.

Another curious piece of water-divining, also among my immediate relations, took place in Friuli in northern Italy; I was not present, but was told of it by my aunt, Miss Jane Day, who was. My cousin Cora Slocomb, who like my mother came from New Orleans, had married a certain Count Detalmo di Brazza, the eldest of a family of seventeen brothers and sisters, of whom the only outstanding member was Count Pierre di Brazza, the explorer, after whom Brazzaville, the capital of the French Congo, is named. Detalmo had inherited large estates in Friuli, and his wife at once set about improving the lot of the peasants on these—starting lace-schools, instructing in hygiene, enforcing morals (or at least marriages) and so on. At one point it was considered desirable to build some new houses, to give better accommodation on one part of the estate, with easier access to work; but at the most suitable spot there was no water, and my American cousin was certainly not going to see houses built without a proper water-supply if she could help it! It so happened that her mother, old Mrs. Slocomb, and my Aunt Jane Day were staying at Brazzà when this project came under discussion, and Mrs. Slocomb arbitrarily demanded (she was always arbitrary) to be shown on the map just where the proposed new village was to be. A large-scale map was produced and spread out in front of the old lady; Aunt Jane said that she took up the long ivory paper-cutter she habitually used (I remember it well) and held it in her fingers over the map. One end of the ivory, after some oscillation, dipped down on the map at a point only a short distance away from the wished-for site. "If you dig there," Aunt Abby said firmly to her son-in-law, "you will find plenty of water, running water, at between fifteen and twenty feet down." Cousin Detalmo didn't really believe her, but he was the courtliest of men, and had plenty of his own labour available; he dug, and there was the water flowing abundantly, just over fifteen feet down—the new hamlet was duly built.

Very odd that it could be done from a map, I find. I never heard that Aunt Abby put this singular gift to use anywhere else, but I suppose she must have known that she could do it. Aunt Jane I may say was the most puritanically truthful of women, always spoiling her family's more lively and impressionistic stories by cutting them down to size—I cannot believe that she invented this episode, and indeed Cousin Detalmo confirmed it to me when, later, I was myself staying at Brazzà.

I imagine that there is in fact no general doubt about water-divining as an activity; but I was interested to learn, from one of the children's nannies, Hilda Comley, of a case of someone actually being *paid* to do it, and by no less a concern than the old Great Western Railway Company. Nurse Comley had an uncle, James Comley, a bricklayer by trade; he lived in Clifton Road,

E

Swindon. His gift was well known locally—the farmers round about always sent for him if they wished to sink a well. He found water for many people at places near Swindon like Wroughton and Brinkworth, and discovered the supply for Foxhill, the late Mr. James White's racing-stables. When the Great Western was starting up its big railway workshops at Swindon, and wanted water for them, James Comley was called in, and duly found it; he was paid a lump sum for doing so. What is more, I believe the railway company paid him a small annual retaining fee to find water for them when called upon; in the days of steam, water in quantity was essential for filling the engines. I can well remember the narrow open tanks, running just alongside the track, from which the engines on long-distance trains scooped up water as they passed, and the whooshing sound it made; at large stations, like Oxford, the tall pipe, with a big rubber or leather tube looped up over it, for filling engines at rest, used to be a familiar sight on a siding. James Comley also found the requisite water for the engine and repair installations at Southall, on the G.W.R.

Another example of a para-normal faculty being used deliberately and professionally is graphology, or reading hand-writing. There is of course a sort of science of this, in which the length of the tails of g's and y's and so on is supposed to indicate something or other—I have never studied it, though I can read hand-writings, but I have good reason for knowing, as I shall presently show, that the real professionals rely much more on the para-normal sense than on the shape of the letters when making reports on a hand-writing, or rather on the character of the writer, for business purposes.

I learned that I could read hand-writing (as I first saw dowsing being practised) at Skipness. It was on my first visit there; one wet evening after tea, Owen and I and all four Grahams—Bertie, Angus, Ethel and Frances—were sitting in the old school-room chatting, when somehow the question of reading people's character from their hand-writing came up. I had never seen any of their writings, of course, except Ethel's—she and I worked together in the C.O.S. office in Chelsea—and they amused themselves by producing non-committal scraps of their own writing and making me read them, one after the other; it was clear from their laughter that I was often being sensationally accurate, though I had no idea whose writing I had in my hand. (It would not have told me much if I *had* known; at that stage they were all, except thel, complete strangers to me.)

What I did when given an envelope, or a slip of paper with a few lines written on it, was first to look rather carefully at the writing and see what it was like—pretty or ugly, neat or sprawly; then I went on looking, till the script became almost blurred, and as I did so the picture of a character somehow formed itself in my mind, and I said what I saw, or found—generally, on that occasion, to loud applause. Presently they took me up to where Aunt Emily was sitting in her small armchair by the drawing-room fire, writing letters on her knee, as was her habit after tea, and pronounced triumphantly that I was a nailer at reading hand-writings. Aunt Emily, always sceptical, promptly handed me an envelope addressed to herself saying—"Well, see what you make of *that*!"

The writing was fairly large, bold and determined; but I found it a rather baffling subject for the exercise of my newly-discovered powers. In fact I think I was tired—reading hand-writings *is* tiring; later I would never attempt more than two or three at one sitting, and by this time I had already read half a dozen or more. What came to me from that envelope was not any sort of person or character, but a room—beautiful in itself, but disfigured with ugly things: ugly cretonnes on the chairs, ugly curtains, hideous ornaments. Rather haltingly, I told what I saw.

"H'm. You don't say whether the writer tells *lies* or not!" said old Mrs. Graham crisply, resuming possession of the envelope; the others laughed. In fact I was to come to know that writing terribly well—the letter was from old Lady O'Malley, some months later to become my mother-in-law. (She did sometimes tell lies, and she was a baffling character. The room I saw was, as I later recognised, the drawing-room at Denton.)

I only remember having one other sensational success in reading hand-writings. During the Peace Conference in 1919, Owen and I were dining one night in Paris with Sidney Waterlow, and Owen happened to mention that I could read people's writings. Sidney instantly whipped out an envelope and handed it across the table to me. This time I was not tired, and the character that emerged, though peculiar and self-contradictory, came through clearly; I described it without hesitation, while Sidney stared in amazement.

"But you might have been brought up with him!" he exclaimed. The writing was that of someone I had never met, and never did meet—Middleton Murry.

More than a quarter of a century later I met a professional graphologist—the well-known Gusti Oesterreicher. It was in 1936; I had taken Patrick and Kate for a skiing holiday in Germany. We stayed at Untergreinau, near Garmisch-Partenkirchen, and often went down the village after supper to spend an evening at the famous Haus Hirth, run as a guest-house, in the most delightful fashion, by the owners, Walther and Hanna Hirth; it was always full of interesting people—actors, writers, musicians— and among them, that year, was Fraülein Oesterreicher—she was formally introduced as "die Graphologin". I was fascinated by this encounter, and talked to her as much as I could; I made no bones about the fact that I was an amateur in the same field myself, and she took a kindly interest, and even tried me out with some written scraps. She explained that for professional purposes it was as well to have the scientific basis, but that in fact she herself relied mainly on what she called the intuitive side. I asked about the professional aspect. Large businesses, Government institutions, and above all banks, all over Germany, when considering appointments to positions of trust would send her specimens of the various applicants' hand-writings, identified only by numbers, and she would give her opinion on the characters of the writers. It was a whole-time job; that was how she gained her livelihood. As in the case of the Swindon water-diviner, I was impressed by the fact that important public concerns, presumably run by highly practical people, were willing to pay out good money for the exercise of a para-normal faculty.

Fraülein Oesterreicher was so nice, and very indulgent to us; she actually volunteered to read anything we would like her opinion of for us, all for free. I had nothing on me that first evening but a letter from William Strang (now Lord Strang)—I gave her the envelope, and watched her while she read it. She was much quicker than I could ever be—almost at once *"Bedeutend begabt!"* (strikingly gifted) she exclaimed; *"Bedeutend begabt!"* she repeated and then, more slowly—*"Aber kein glücklicher Mensch."* An evening or two later I managed to find a non-committal scrap of Patrick's hand-writing, and tried her with that; of course it was probably very immature—he was only eighteen then—but his life has not turned out at all along the lines that Gusti suggested.

I never asked Gusti Oesterreicher whether she thought that having the actual piece of paper, which the writer's hand had touched, in her own hand had anything to do with reading the writing on it; I wish now that I had. Of course thirty years ago photographing documents was not as common as it is today, but I should like to know whether she would have found a Xerox-ed piece of writing as easy to read as the original. I am fairly certain that she would not. Material things do seem to have a capacity for carrying a certain "impress"—I do not know how else to express it—derived from a person, and perceptible by another person: as that room and bed at Blois carried the impression of Mrs. Simpson's desperation. And apparently there is often—though by no means always—a material base for apparitions, as will be seen in the next section.

There is one other deliberate exercise of para-normal faculties for practical purposes to which I think reference should be made—the use of the pendulum. I have never attempted it myself; it seems to be nearer to dowsing than to anything else, and as I am such a poor hand at dowsing, I haven't bothered. But my son Patrick uses it with excellent results, some of which I will now record.

I should first explain how the pendulum works. Any small solid object is suspended from a silk cord, one end of which is then held in the hand so that the object can swing free; Patrick uses his signet-ring, but it need not be a precious metal, or indeed metal at all—a heavy wooden curtain-ring would do. The cord, however, must be of silk: man-made fibres, or even the innocent vegetables hemp or manila, fashioned into string, will not extract the pendulum's secrets. I find this charming—silk, like honey, has a sort of unique naturalness, an untouchable purity; it does not seem to me strange that silk alone will release whatever mysterious power provides the answers to questions addressed to the pendulum—surely akin to the power which so agitates the hazel-twig in the dowser's hands?

These questions must be carefully framed, because the pendulum can only answer Yes or No. Patrick, holding the silken cord in his hand, first asks the pendulum—"How are you going to say Yes?" The signet-ring begins to swing in a circle, anti-clockwise, quite unmistakably. He thanks it; then—"Good. And how are you going to say No?" The ring hangs immobile.

So much for the procedure. Now I will mention some of the pendulum's helpful activities.

At one point Patrick wished to move out into the country to

live, but because of his work he had to be within easy reach of Oxford. He enquired of several house-agents, but could hear of nothing suitable. A friend suggested that he should consult the pendulum. He asked it, in the first instance, if there was a house for him?—it answered "Yes". Then, with the map spread out, he asked in turn—"Is it to the North? To the South? To the East? To the West?" In each case the answer was No, the ring stubbornly remaining motionless. Rather frustrated, he nevertheless persevered: "To the South-east? South-west?" and so on; still No, till he came to the North-east, when the ring moved vigorously in its circle. Encouraged, he began the rather complicated questioning necessary to pinpoint the situation of his new house. "Is it as much as ten miles out?" No. "As much as nine?" and so on, till he thought he had established that the distance was roughly nine miles. On the map the only sign of habitation at that distance was marked "Alchester—Roman town"; to this unpromising locality he proceeded to drive, hoping that there might be a farm-house or cottage near by that was to let. There was not—there was nothing! He had taken the map and the silk cord with him; now, by the roadside, he set up the pendulum, reproved it gently for misleading him, and then asked it—"Is the house near Oxford?" "Yes." "Is it eight miles?" "No." "Seven miles?" "Yes."

He looked again at the map. Seven miles to the North-east of Oxford lies the small town of Islip—so he firmly asked—"Is the house in Islip?" A vigorous Yes was the response. Now much more encouraged he drove back towards Islip; when he reached the outskirts he stopped at each turning and enquired of the pendulum, "Do I turn left?" No. "Do I turn right?" Yes. So directed, step by step as it were, he found himself in a small street with some oldish houses on one side, and a brand new and rather attractive little housing estate on the other, rows of attached houses round two sides of an open grassy square.

Now comes an odd thing. Patrick had asked the pendulum

originally whether the house that was waiting for him was old or new, and by the usual complicated series of questions had learned that it was between two and three hundred years old. So now he naturally asked if it was one of the old houses on the opposite side of the street? No. "Is it one of those new houses?" Yes. Incredulous, he drove on to the new estate, left the car in the neat parking-place, and set out to make enquiries. Through an open window he saw a man in shirt-sleeves, and asked him if by any chance there was a house to let?

"Funny thing you should ask that," said the man. "My neighbour has just heard that his firm are sending him to Glasgow, and he wants to find someone to take over his lease." And in that neighbour's house Patrick is now living!

Then why did the pendulum say that the house was between two and three centuries old? If you ask any of the good folk of Islip the way to the housing estate by its new fancy name they will eventually say—"Oh, you mean the Old Farm!" The neat little modern houses are built on the site of a farm that had stood there for nearly three hundred years. I suppose a pendulum can get a bit muddled when new houses are built on an old site, especially when they are faced largely with the original stone from the old building, as happened in this case—anyhow no one is going to complain about a little thing like that, if he is led in under twenty-four hours to precisely the house he wants.

The pendulum doesn't seem to mind helping in the smallest matters. Some time after they moved in my daughter-in-law lost her spectacles. She hunted for them all through the house and even in the car; they were nowhere to be found. In desperation— she needed them for her work, and had already missed the first bus into Oxford, and there was only one other—she asked Patrick to get the pendulum to help. (He was ill at this time, and unable to drive the car.) He asked it about the kitchen and the drawing-room, the two likeliest places; it said No to both. Rather hopelessly, he asked if the spectacles were in the dining-room, a most improbable place—the result was a vigorous Yes. But then Patrick remembered that the previous evening she had had the steps in, to do something to the dining-room curtains; he fetched them again, and looked on the top of a high cupboard by the window—there, sure enough, the spectacles were.

And there was the matter of the return of the cat. They have a much-cherished young cat—very individualistic, like all cats, but beautiful and intelligent. Because they were rather concerned about an inexperienced cat in a new locality, full of strange cats, not all of them friendly, they trained it to be let out early in the evening, then come in and have its supper, and remain indoors all night; it was quite accustomed to this routine, and normally adhered to it. One night, however, it failed to come back at the proper time; they were already getting a little anxious when suddenly a violent thunderstorm came on, with a fierce downpour. Patrick adores the cat, and was so worried that eventually he asked the pendulum if the creature was under cover? Yes, it was. Somewhat relieved, he asked whether it was in a cottage?—a barn?—the pub?—the church?—the pendulum said "No" to every suggestion. (He thinks it may well have been under a car; it loves sitting under cars even in fine weather.) It was now ten past ten, and they wanted to go to bed; they have to make a very early start for work in the morning—so he asked the pendulum, with the usual circumlocutions, what time the cat would get in, and established that it would be back at latest by 10.25. Patrick stayed up for it; the rain had taken off, and he opened the french window into the garden, and sat and waited. Ten-fifteen—no cat; ten-twenty—still no cat. The minutes ticked by while he sat, looking out, where the light from the window shone across the small rain-soaked garden. At twenty-four-and-a-half minutes past ten the animal came bounding over the low wall beyond the lawn and fairly raced into the house, as if pursued. But no enemy cat was in pursuit; it was as if some strange compulsion was driving it to be in time. It was quite dry.

Patrick always thanks the pendulum for its help; he treats it with decent respect. He never asks it for any immediate personal gain, like which horse will win the Derby; only for needed help, like being led to a house, or retrieving his wife's spectacles. In fact it seems to have a fairly strong sense of self-respect. On one occasion some disbelieving friends asked him to show what it could do, and began asking it frivolous questions—it flatly refused to answer, even to show how it would say Yes or No.

PART IV

Apparitions—some first-hand accounts

Apparitions

I hasten to say that I have never seen a ghost, never heard mysterious footsteps, never felt a sudden inexplicable chill. But I do not think that it is possible to omit the subject of apparitions altogether, if one is considering the para-normal faculty: too many wholly reputable people have had these experiences. And I have myself seen the effect on animals of something invisible to the ordinary human being, in more than one place.

It has already been mentioned that when I was a child we lived near Windsor Great Park, in which we rode constantly; the village was called Eaglefield Green. To reach the Park from our house, before a new road was built—on my father's initiative—we had to cross the top of the Green itself, an open furzy stretch, and join a road which ran up the farther side to Bishop's Gate, the nearest entrance to the Park. On the left of this road was a broad grass verge, some thirty feet wide, along which we cantered our ponies; but at one particular spot they always shied violently—to the point of leaving the grass for the road. Even when Hall, the coachman, ordained that we were to trot along the road itself just there, instead of cantering on the grass, the animals still shied. There was nothing to be seen, and I never heard any story of a catastrophe on "The Green"—but there was some presence there which frightened the creatures.

Another place where I have seen animals noticeably affected by something wholly invisible and inaudible to human beings was at

Government House in the Isle of Man. During World War II, when Lord Granville was Governor, I had to go and give some lectures in Douglas, and Lady Granville very kindly asked me to stay with them instead of at an hotel. Lord Granville was an enormous man, over six feet tall and immensely broad—in the Navy he had been known as "Wisp Granville"; he kept dogs of a very unusual breed, black chows, to which he was devoted. Their food was brought into the dining-room in the evening, but he would always cut it up and dish it out himself, putting each dog's bowl on a piece of linoleum under a side-table—Lady Granville insisted on the linoleum to spare the polished floor. However, the dogs were not fed until the humans had practically finished their meal; they lay, patient and dignified, behind their master's chair, waiting. But I noticed that in the course of dinner, every night, and long before feeding-time, they would all get up, slowly, growling, and walk in a menacing fashion towards a french window which gave on to the garden; Lord Granville would curtly order them back to their places. Of course with the chows one could not see if their hackles rose—their shining black ruffs were too huge; but it was quite clear that something was upsetting them, and one night I asked my host what it was?—the french window was curtained, so there was nothing to be seen.

"Oh, it's only Lord So-and So," Lord Granville said cheerfully; "he always comes in about this time"—and went on to explain that Lord So-and-So had been a former Governor of the island, and lived in the house. With another predecessor, however, the chows were very friendly indeed; when we were sitting having tea in the garden, on the far side of the lawn, they would suddenly jump up, race across towards the french window, and greet some invisible person with gentle welcoming barks—and then follow him, walking up and down, up and down, on the flagged path which ran along under the house, sniffing at the level at which the hands of a tall man would hang, if he walked with

them dangling at his side—it was most uncanny to watch them.
I had some trouble in getting to Douglas on that, my first visit;
I was to go by boat from Fleetwood, and of course had my tickets,
but when I made to go on board an official asked to see my passport. This was a facer—it had never occurred to me that I should
need a passport for the Isle of Man, and I had left mine in London.
But so it was: Regulation 18B was in full force, and many of the
detainees under it were kept in the Isle of Man; no one could go
there without a passport. Oh, there was a fuss. I got hold of some
high police official, and persuaded him to ring up Owen who,
mercifully, was in the Foreign Office at that time, and settled that
he should ring up the Governor and somehow arrange that I
might be allowed ashore—which presumably was how Lady
Granville knew that I was coming. Lord Granville then kindly
telephoned to the police at Fleetwood, and I was allowed aboard;
on arrival at Douglas The Deemster himself, no less, came to
meet the boat, flourishing some document, and I was allowed to
land. This was all very exciting—I had no idea that there really
was such a person as The Deemster; but there he was, a brisk
little man, who took me in his car and insisted on driving me
round the course of the T.T. motor-cycle race, over the mountain,
before depositing me at Government House. That was rather too
exciting: The Deemster drove immensely fast, and took most
of the many blind bends on the wrong side; I was really quite glad
when the drive was over.

Some years later, when England was still suffering from innum-
erable restrictions, there came into fashion a rhyme which ran—

> "Take me away from The People,
> Back to the Isle of Man!
> I'd be far more free
> Under 18B
> Than as part of the Postwar Plan."

This jingle was purely sardonic in intention, but all unwittingly it contained more than a grain of truth; the arrangements made for the large bulk of the detainees were the most civilised it is possible to imagine. Instead of shutting them up in barracks or draughty hutments, the authorities simply took over a small sea-side resort, Port Erin, on the west side of the island, fenced it in with a ten-foot barrier of barbed wire, put the detainees inside, and left them there. This was not difficult to do, since Port Erin lies at the head of a fairly long, fairly narrow bay; patrol-boats guarded this, and there were guards at both ends of the fence, and at the entrance, where the road from Castletown comes in. But inside—as I saw for myself when Lord Granville (who liked to visit the place periodically) took me there one day—life went on perfectly normally; the detainees were out shopping, or having coffee in the little tea-shops, or just strolling along the sea-front; there was a cinema or the Marine Museum for entertainment, and some form of church for worship. It was a revelation of imagination and humane common sense on someone's part.

I came across another example of imagination and humane treatment of detainees on the island, and for this the Governor himself was largely responsible. I wished to visit the Museum, because the Isle of Man is one of the few other places in the British Isles where tombstones with interlaced ornament, so characteristic of the West Highlands (of which Uncle Robert Graham had made those plaster casts on Islay and in Mull) are to be found; I hoped the Curator would be able to tell me the most convenient places nearby where I could see some. He was, and ultimately I did visit one or two graveyards—but what was really exciting him at the moment, the only thing he wanted to talk about, was the excavation of three Celtic chieftains' houses which was currently taking place near Arbory; they had only been discovered fairly recently. Now among the unfortunate Central Europeans who had happened to be in Britain at the outbreak of war, and were therefore incarcerated under Regulation 18B, was the eminent German archaeologist Dr. Gerhardt Bersu; he had been lecturing, was picked up, and sent to the Isle of Man. Some compassionate genius in the British Government told Lord Granville that Bersu and other interned German scholars should be allowed if possible to use their brains; Lord Granville and the then Attorney-General for the Island, a certain Mr. Ramsay Moore (who was and is an ardent supporter of the Museum), decided that Bersu's brains would be best employed excavating the new site. So out he went, with a team of helpers and an armed escort, and dug away—for the princely remuneration of 6d. a day! The doctor and his team had already found enough evidence to make a beautiful, detailed and perfectly accurate model of one of these structures—the Curator showed it to me, and later I went back and was shown it in even more detail by the old German himself.

This was an inspired arrangement—the site was dug, at a time when manpower was hard to come by, by cheerful labour, practically free of charge, and dug under the most expert possible supervision; Dr. Bersu did not in the least mind being watched over at his work by at least one armed sentry, and spent a useful and contented war—everyone was happy.

But on the way back from that visit to the detainee centre at Port Erin I came across evidence of an apparition, an animal one this time. Lord Granville was extremely well-informed about his island, and interested in every aspect of it; he usually drove himself, and as we hummed along the quiet roads he would point out any object of interest, and tell me all about it. A considerable stretch of the road between Castletown and Douglas had been widened and remade some time before; as we approached a fine new bridge the Governor said suddenly—"This bridge used to be haunted."

"Not really?"

"Fact. By a spotted dog—people didn't much like it."

F

Of course I pressed for the story; he gave it, in the brief clipped sentences he always used. A spotted dog was frequently seen on the old bridge; when the road was being widened extra land had to be taken in, just here, from the grounds of a house on the left, including what had been the owners' dogs cemetery; the workmen had been startled to find that the skeleton of one dog wore a metal collar and chain. The skeleton was sent to the Museum at Castletown to be examined; the collar and chain proved to be of silver, the skeleton that of a hyena! But having been dug up, the spotted dog apparently no longer "walked" on the new bridge.

I was charmed by this, and would have liked to discuss and theorise about why the removal of the skeleton should have "laid" the apparition; but naval men are not, in my experience, great ones for theorising—instead I asked—

"Lord Granville, have you ever seen a ghost?"

"Yes," he said instantly. "Saw one in my study yesterday afternoon, at twenty to three."

I suppose thousands of people have been asked that question; I wonder if it ever received a more prompt and categorical reply? The ghost was of an old woman, small and neatly dressed in dark grey, I learned on enquiring further; she came into that room fairly frequently, sometimes carrying what appeared to be a tray —at first when Lord Granville saw her he had assumed that it was one of the maids; and he now presumed that it was the phantom of some elderly servant. But all enquiries had failed to establish her identity, or why she should continue to bring a ghostly tray into the Governor's study.

A more interesting apparition of an attendant is what in my husband's youth was known in South Oxfordshire as The Waterperry Ghost—quite a modern one. While the Henley family, whom the O'Malleys knew well, were still living at Waterperry, old Mr. Henley died after a long illness, during which he was faithfully looked after by a trained nurse; to make things easier for the household one of the ground-floor sitting-rooms was transformed into the sickroom, and there, after months of suffering, he at last died. When the room reverted to its normal use it was presently noticed that the figure of a nurse, in cap and apron, was frequently to be seen moving about the room, always silently—if spoken to she did not reply. But what was curious was that the figure had no face! Now during the last years of his life Mr. Henley had become quite blind; the poor old gentleman, as blind people will, used to reassure himself of the nurse's presence, it would seem, by gently touching her—but his Victorian courtesy and modesty would not allow him to touch her face. If, as seems probable, it was his recollected dependence which ultimately projected her image into the room, he would obviously have remembered, from the days when he had his sight, what a trained nurse (such as his wife's monthly nurses) looked like; but the face of the woman who meant so much to him he had never seen, and so he could not recall it.

Another case of a sitting-room used as a bedroom I have already recorded in my life of my mother; for the sake of completeness I will repeat it here. During her girlhood in New Orleans, soon after the Civil War, she went to stay on a plantation house out in the country; like many other such houses it was built round a central hall, and though deep verandahs shaded all the rooms, in the heat of summer it was the habit of the ladies of the household to sit in this hall for coolness; they sewed and chatted, or someone read aloud—as they had done throughout the war. Now to this house had been sent during the war a prisoner, a young Northern officer who had lost the use of both his legs and was permanently disabled; his enemy hostess went to the trouble of procuring for him a bathchair which could be self-propelled by an outer band along the wheels and, like old Mr. Henley, he was given a room on the ground floor, so that he could move about freely. He stayed on the plantation till he died—part of his stay was in the summer, and it had become his habit, during the long hot afternoons, to wheel himself to his bedroom door, open it, and propel his chair out into the hall, where he sat near the women at their war-time tasks of picking lint and rolling bandages, silently securing companionship. My mother knew nothing of all this, and she was surprised when several times, as they sat there, one of the doors off the hall opened of itself; on one occasion she got up to shut it.

"Don't do that," said the mistress of the house; "it's only Lieutenant So-and-So. And if he was happy enough here to want to come and sit with us when he was sick and a prisoner, he shall come and sit with us now, if he cares to."

PART V

Telepathy—experiments and telepathic dreams

Telepathy

I imagine that the para-normal faculty about which ordinary people have fewest doubts or reservations is telepathy, which the *Oxford English Dictionary* admirably defines as "the communication of impressions from one mind to another, independently of the recognised channels of sense". This power, or gift, unlike dreams or what I have called "knowings", can easily be checked and verified, and has been the subject of endless carefully controlled experiments, so that it is more or less recognised and accepted. But what is so tiresome about these experiments is that they seem nearly always to be conducted with playing-cards, which in themselves are so very uninteresting; I can never understand how the person with telepathic powers, when these are being tested, has the patience to go on and on saying that the next card in the pack will be the ten of clubs or the ace of spades, or whatever it is. There are surely other tests which are just as verifiable, and not quite so boring; one such we used to use at Skipness, where Frances Graham, besides her skill as a dowser, displayed a marked power of telepathy with one or two people—best of all with my husband.

This was our form of test, which was often put on for the entertainment of the house-party. Frances would be sent out of the room—we usually played the telepathy game, as we called it, in the drawing-room after dinner—with a companion to invigilate her; they went into the library, some distance along the gallery, and shut the door. Someone in the drawing-room was then asked to take a book out of the bookcase, open it, and choose a paragraph, or at least a sentence; the name of the book and the number of the page was given to the assembled company, including Owen, and the sentence read out; the page number and the sentence were written down and put in a blotter. Someone then opened the door and called for Frances to return, which she did, still escorted by her companion; Owen went over and stood by her in silence. After a few moments she used to take his hand, and then—sometimes quickly and with assurance, sometimes more hesitantly—she would move to the bookcase, and still holding his hand take out the book, lay it on a table, and turn the pages with her free hand till she came to the right one; sometimes she would say the number aloud and ask "Is that right?" "Yes," someone told her. Then—obviously this was the most difficult part—she would look at the page, perhaps murmuring "It's near the bottom," to herself, and at last would come out with the chosen sentence. She and Owen were always standing in a brightly-lit room, in full view of us all; if there had been any question of his nodding or shaking his head, or otherwise helping her in her search for the book we could not have failed to see it—in fact I am satisfied that he did nothing of the sort. Sceptical visitors—in particular the late Sir Charles Darwin, who was intensely sceptical; he was a frequent guest—in fact often used to get up and stand close to them to watch their every movement, but greatly to his annoyance he could never detect anything that Owen did that might have helped Frances in the least. "There must be *some-thing*," he used to say, irritably; of course there was, the tele-pathic power, only he didn't like to acknowledge its existence.

After my sensational success in reading hand-writing, the Grahams insisted that I should try my hand at finding a book and the chosen sentence—I tried with Frances, with Ethel, and also with Owen, but always without any success. And it interested me that though Frances could, somewhat rarely, find a book or pick up a paper-knife, or even a flower in a vase, without holding his hand, she could never succeed in finding a particular page or passage without touching him.

I have another record of touch as a factor in telepathic impressions, from my sister-in-law Margery O'Malley. She married a clergyman, the Reverend Sidney Scarlett Smith (a great-nephew of Sir James Scarlett of Crimea fame) a most devout and sobersided person. In 1916 he was Rector of Hampton Bishop, a village on the River Wye outside Hereford, and one day while "parishing", as he called visiting his flock, a farmers' wife, a Mrs. Christopher Field, gave him an account of her father's death-bed; Margery wrote it in her diary that same day, 13 December 1916. I quote her entry.

"There were present, besides the dying man, Polly Field herself, her sister, her own husband, and also the curate of the parish. Suddenly she heard the tune of *Rock of Ages* being played. This hymn was her father's favourite and one which he had frequently desired her to sing or repeat to him. The music was the most beautiful she had ever heard and came from a distance. It was played (she asserted) upon 'a harp and a bugle'! Both she and the dying man heard it. She asked her sister if she could hear it, but she could not till Polly touched her; then, however, she could hear it distinctly. In the same way Christopher could not hear it till she touched him. Then he could hear it."

Telepathy seems not to be confined to deliberate efforts; dreams can also convey a telepathic message, or, as the *O.E.D.* prudently says, "impression". I can give one curious instance of an impression—but no message—being conveyed by one person to not one, but *two* others, through a dream. During the first war, in 1917, my husband and I, as has already been mentioned, were living in The Holt at Godalming, which Ruth and George Mallory had lent to us while he was in France. Frances Graham was by this time married to Cosmo Gordon of Ellon; he was in the Guards, and was also in France; she was living with her mother at Skipness. One night Owen was greatly alarmed by a dream about Frances: she was in some grave danger or distress, though the dream did not specify what form this took. He was, however, sufficiently worried to write to her at Skipness, mentioning the cause of his concern, and asking if she was all right? After a considerable delay he received the following very characteristic reply, on a postcard.

"Thanks for kind dream. My subconscious must have been on the rampage that night, for Cos wrote from St. Omer on the same day, in the same sense. But I am quite all right."

And indeed subsequent careful checking made it clear that Cosmo's dream had also been of some distress or danger which threatened her. Neither she nor Aunt Emily could think of any grounds for this—they were living peacefully at Skipness, their worst difficulty rationing; and even this, on a large estate in Scotland, with a home farm, and an abundance of fish and game, was less of a worry than in most places. All the same I cannot but think that some peril which never materialised must have brushed her with its wing. Anyhow, I record the episode for what it is worth, pointless as it must seem.

Another telepathic dream, which, however, was far from pointless, I feel I must record—though I had it at one remove. It was told to me by the Reverend H. P. Cronshaw, for long the Vicar of St. Marks, North Audley Street—he married us there on Crispin Crispian's Day, 1913. It was told to him by the dreamer himself, another Anglican parson, the late Archdeacon Bevan.

Bevan, at the time of this dream, was Rector of St. Luke's, Chelsea; he was a close friend of Dr. Haig-Brown, who had been headmaster of the Charterhouse School in London. When it was decided to move the school part of the ancient foundation down to the country, near Godalming, Dr. Haig-Brown was already too old and frail to undertake such an effort—a new headmaster was appointed, but the old man was allowed to live out his last years in the Charterhouse itself, with his wife, and a chaplain to conduct the services in the chapel. He was ailing for a long time, and Bevan went regularly to read aloud to him—he read very beautifully, Mr. Cronshaw said.

At last the old man died, and Mrs. Haig-Brown wrote to Bevan to ask him, as an old Carthusian and one whose reading had been pleasant and a comfort to the late doctor to read the lesson at the funeral, which he willingly undertook to do. The night before the funeral he had a most vivid dream. He was standing in the chancel of the Charterhouse Chapel, which was full of a black-clad congregation; opposite him, in another stall, stood Mr. Le Bas, the chaplain. Every detail of the chapel, which Bevan had not seen since his schooldays, was perfectly clear to him. When the time for reading the lesson approached he left his stall and went to the lectern to find the place in the Bible, but there *was* no Bible!—the lectern was bare. Startled and disconcerted, he stepped across to Le Bas and whispered to him "There's no book!" To this Le Bas replied shortly—"There never is." Baffled, Bevan went back to the lectern and stood wondering what to do. At last he returned to Le Bas and asked him urgently—"Then what do you do?" Gruffly, as before, Le Bas whispered—"We always say it by heart!" Frustrated, the unhappy Archdeacon again went back to the lectern, and tried to remember the words of the lesson, but failed. In desperation, he forced himself to approach the unhelpful chaplain for the third time, and asked him —"How does it begin?" Le Bas gave him the opening words, he went back to the empty lectern, and with an effort managed to recite the whole lesson except for one verse, in which he faltered.

That was the end of the dream; but it had made such a deep

and frightening impression on the Archdeacon that next day, not surprisingly, he decided to go to the funeral provided with a book of his own, and took a small Book of Common Prayer with him. At the Charterhouse he and Mr. Le Bas robed in the vestry, and then walked in procession into the chapel. There, all was as in the dream of the night before, with the chapel full of people in black; Bevan of course immediately glanced at the lectern—yes, there was the Bible in position, with the fringed markers hanging down. But he had tucked his prayer-book into his cassock, and still under the influence of that agonising dream, before moving to the lectern he drew it out from under his surplice, took it with him, and placing it on the open Bible, read the lesson, not from the big volume, but from his familiar little book.

When the service was over, and he and Le Bas were unrobing in the vestry, a note was brought him from Mrs. Haig-Brown, asking him to go across and have a cup of tea with her, which of course he did. After thanking him warmly for coming to perform this last service for his old friend she said—"And I cannot tell you how thankful I was that you read it from the Authorised Version. My husband never could get to like the Revised Version. I did think of asking Mr. Le Bas if the Authorised Version could not be used, but he prefers the Revised Version, and he doesn't like any alteration in his arrangements. But—you may think me very weak—but I lay awake much of last night wishing that I had the courage to ask him to let the Authorised Version be used today."

(When Archdeacon Bevan recounted this tale to his family, they insisted on his trying again to say the lesson by heart, to them. He did it quite successfully, except that he again hesitated at the verse in which he had faltered in the dream.)

But surely no one can doubt the telepathic element here? Le Bas's grumpiness and stubbornness transmitted from the City of London to Chelsea in such a highly dramatised form.

A friend of ours who rather frequently had dreams with a

telepathic content—or at least an informative content—was Sir Bertrand Jerram. We saw a good deal of him during the Spanish Civil War, when he was, first, in France with the evacuated remains of the Embassy to Madrid (of which my husband was placed in charge on his return from the Legation in Mexico in 1938) and then in Spain, where he was Number Two in the Agency at Burgos, where Sir Robert Hodgson was Britain's accredited representative to General Franco. We were constantly dodging in and out to Burgos for consultations, and did some splendid jaunts into the surrounding countryside with Jerram. (Nobody ever used his Christian name, that I heard.) He told the two dreams that follow to my husband, who wrote them down; I quote from his account.

"Jerram was at Burgos when he got a telegram from his sister in Cornwall saying that his mother had had a stroke and that if he wished to see her alive he should return at once.

"As it happened he was due to fly to Warsaw that very day. He consulted me as to what he should do, and it was decided that he should still fly to Warsaw, and after a day and a night there fly to Croydon and take a charter plane from Croydon to Cornwall. (This was before the days of Heathrow.)

"During the night he spent in Warsaw he dreamed very vividly —as was indeed natural—of his mother; in his dream his mother's conversation was largely directed to all the horrors which at this time (1938) were going on in the world. 'Why,' she said to Jerram in the dream, holding in her hand the old copy of Hymns Ancient and Modern which was in use in the family as long as he could remember, 'why can we not turn our thoughts for a time to what is lovely and delightful—to flowers and spring and the beauties of nature and the goodness still to be found in human beings?' At this point Jerram woke up; and in the moment of waking, heard a voice which was neither his own, nor his mother's, repeat with the utmost clarity and distinction the opening lines of the hymn—

There is a land of pure delight
Where saints immortal reign . . .

"When he reached Cornwall his mother was still alive, but as a result of the stroke she could only speak very imperfectly, and her daughters were concerned because they could not understand something that she was trying to say. A meeting of the village Mother's Union, over which Mrs. Jerram normally presided, was due to take place in the house within the next few days; at these gatherings at least one hymn was usually sung, and her daughters assumed that the message which the old lady was vainly trying to get across must be concerned with the hymn for the next meeting, since the only word which they could identify, in her garbled speech, was 'saint' or 'saints'. Mrs. Jerram was becoming more and more insistent, and more and more irritable at her failure to make herself understood, and they had searched the book of Hymns A. & M. for hymns about special saints, and endeavoured to ascertain if any of these were what was in their mother's head; but nothing that they showed her satisfied her, and her impatience and distress mounted. On his arrival Jerram was told all this—he got hold of the tattered old A. & M. hymnbook which he had seen in his dream, and looked out the hymn which begins 'There is a land of pure delight . . .' and there of course he discovered the references to all the things which his mother in his dream in Warsaw had suggested should be dwelt on. He showed the hymn to the old lady, who at once made it perfectly plain that she was at last satisfied and at peace in her mind.

"And of course a few days later that hymn was duly sung at the Mother's Union meeting."

The other dream of Jerram's which my husband wrote down was more mundane, but perhaps worth recording.

Before he became Ambassador to Chile, Jerram was Minister

in Sweden, and on very friendly terms with the late King. Race-meetings in Sweden generally took place on Sundays; and on a certain Saturday night Jerram had a very vivid dream that he was at one—he was anxious to place his bets, but was impeded by the crowd from getting anywhere near the tote. At this point he turned round and found the old King jammed next to him in the crowd. Together they climbed over some iron railings and managed to get to the box where bets were made. Jerram knew nothing about the horses, but the King said, "You just put your money on Mandalay; he is an outsider, but I am sure he will win."

So much for the dream. Next day Jerram went out to the races in the afternoon, and as usual sat in the diplomatic box; looking over the shoulder of the man in front of him he was shocked to see on the latter's newspaper, in banner headlines—"Death of the King".

Jerram realised that he must leave at once, but he hurriedly ascertained that there was a horse running at longish odds, called not Mandalay but Manderley. He pushed all the money he had brought with him—nearly £100—into the hands of a friend with urgent instructions at all costs to put the lot on Manderley. Then he left the racecourse to call on his Swedish colleagues to condole, and to concert arrangements for a memorial service in the English church.

Manderley won and Jerram made nearly £1,000.

The last dream I shall mention brings me back to the *Oxford English Dictionary*'s definition of telepathy, "the communication of impressions from one mind to another"—"impressions" and "mind" being the important words. I am not sure whether scientists now credit animals with having *minds*; as they have brains, it seems fair to assume that they have something corresponding to a mind. Anyhow this dream was the communication of an impression, and a very strong impression too, from a cat to its owner.

Since this is such an unusual occurrence, some account of the human being concerned is called for. Phyllis Broome was the younger daughter of Edward Broome, a business man from the Midlands; he lived at Areley Kings near Stourport in Worcestershire; in the winter he rode regularly to hounds, in the summer he went and climbed in Switzerland, and was a long-standing and eminent member of the Alpine Club. In his day he had done some very good climbs in many parts of the Alps, but during his latter years, when he was no longer equal to long expeditions, he usually spent most of his time at Zermatt, doing short easy scrambles on the Riffelhorn, or glacier walks, with his guides. Like most elderly members of the Alpine Club he always stayed at M. Seiler's famous hotel, the *Monte Rosa*; and there, in the summer of 1907, we met him and his daughter, who accompanied him on these summer trips to look after his well-being; she did not climb. "Old Broome", as the rising generation like Geoffrey Winthrop Young and George Mallory called him, was the most hard-headed, down-to-earth person imaginable; he was good-natured, but even his kindness was salted with mockery. His daughter Phyllis was cast in the same mould, though she had a much more active intelligence than her parent, and her interests ranged further afield than hunting and mountaineering; casual, cool, amusing and amused, she sat on The Wall, as the terrace outside the *Monte Rosa* was called, watching the climbers come and go with a slightly ironical eye, listening with a rather sceptical amusement to the flood of gossip which inundated Zermatt during the climbing season.

We made friends that first year; during the two following summers, when we again put in a couple of weeks (all we could afford) at Zermatt, it was a pleasure to find Phyllis Broome there —one was sure of entertainment on off days. She looked after me when I went down with dysentery with the utmost kindness, but rallied me mercilessly about some of the middle-aged A.C. men who took a fancy to me.

I cannot now remember whether it was in 1908 or 1909 that she told me one morning, in some distress, of her dream about her cat the previous night. Phyllis had a much-loved, rather elderly cat, on which she lavished a more uncritical affection than I ever knew her give to any human friend; when she and her father went abroad in the summer the cat went on holiday too, accompanying the housemaid (also elderly) to her home some forty miles away in a hamper. The cat had done this for several years, and was quite accustomed to the procedure; it liked the housemaid; there was never any trouble. But that morning Phyllis told me that she had had a painfully vivid dream of the cat, all wet and muddy, its fur plastered to its body, mewing piteously, plainly in great distress. She was so upset that I suggested she should write to the housemaid to enquire.

"No," she said decidedly, "I shall telegraph." And telegraph she did, reply paid, from Zermatt to Worcestershire—not only to the housemaid at her home, but to the housekeeper at Areley Kings as well, since if the cat had left its temporary abode it would presumably have made for its own home.

At that point I set off with my brother Harry to climb some mountain, an overnight job—we walked up to a hut in the late afternoon, slept there, did our climb, and got back so late for dinner next day that after a bath I had supper in bed. So it was only on the following day that I learned from Phyllis what had become of the cat. She heard first from Areley Kings—the cat was there, and quite safe, the housekeeper telegraphed. Later came an agonised wire from the wretched housemaid—pussy had escaped. But when letters, in due course, reached Zermatt giving full details, the course of events became clear. The cat had arrived back at Areley Kings the day after Phyllis Broome had her distressing dream, and just as it had appeared in the dream—soaking

G

wet (after a series of thunderstorms) muddy and dishevelled, and very unhappy; the housekeeper had succoured it, and so felt able to send the reassuring telegram. Why, for the first time in its life, it had decided to leave the housemaid's care and make for home no one could imagine, and it is not really important; but that in its distress it should have sought its mistress is natural enough— cats do turn to the person who does most for them when upset or alarmed, as any cat-owner will confirm.

It is easy for the sceptic to say that Miss Broome's dream on that particular night was merely a coincidence. Perhaps. Or perhaps cats do have minds, and the *Oxford English Dictionary* has got something!

PART VI

Various Experiences

Various Experiences

There are some para-normal experiences which do not fit neatly into any precise category, since they are neither dreams, nor obviously telepathic, nor the deliberate summoning-up of supra-normal powers; yet I feel that they should be put on record, if they happened to a reputable person, and were related to, or written down by, someone equally reliable. To certain people they seem to happen with great frequency; to others only once or twice in a lifetime. I will begin with two which were experienced by the late the Rev. E. E. Holmes, afterwards Archdeacon of London—than which it is difficult, surely, to *be* more reputable? After some years of parish work, partly in Jarrow, he became chaplain to the then Bishop of Oxford; living at Cuddesdon, he made friends with the O'Malleys, as most of the chaplains did. He was particularly kind to my husband when a schoolboy, and to his sister Eva, taking them for long bicycle-rides in the unspoilt South Oxfordshire countryside, and showing them churches or anything else of interest; they were very fond of him. He was still chaplain when Owen went up to Magdalen, and it was about this time that my sister-in-law, Margery, reports in her diary as follows:

Aug. 13. 1906. Dr. Wilson and Mr. Holmes to dinner. Extraordinary stories. Have written to Owen the ones about the Lectern, and the cheque from India. Will tell here the ones of the Sovereign and the Priest.

1.) Mr. Holmes was walking one day in a street in Jarrow. He was hastening to catch a train, when suddenly he felt himself caught (as it were by something invisible) and forced to walk across the road. It was a broad muddy road and opposite was a large public-house. He had no idea why he walked across the road, but the moment he reached the further pavement he saw glittering on it a sovereign. He picked it up, put it in his pocket, and went on to his train. On his return in the evening a woman came to see him in great distress. She told him that for some considerable time past her son had been out of work. A week before this day he had got work once more, and on this Saturday morning had received his first wages. To her he had given a sovereign to get their goods out of pawn; she had taken in her hand the sovereign and the pawn-tickets, but alas! when she reached the pawn-brokers there was nothing in her hand but the tickets.

In her sad distress of mind and bitter disappointment the woman came to the one man in Jarrow who would believe her tale, and would be both willing and able to help her in her loss—and he was the man who had found her coin, and now handed it back to her.

2.) One evening, he was returning to his house, very tired, when he was arrested by a sudden thought about a house which he was passing. The thought was as a voice which, without sound, said to him "Stop—go to that house—go in." He stepped across, raised the knocker of the door—then paused. "How absurd!" said he to himself. "What have I to go upon? What a fool I shall look. It is nothing—I am tired. I will go home." He put the knocker down again noiselessly, and went home.

Next day, partly out of curiosity, he went back to the house. The fanlight was darkened by a cloth—in Jarrow the sign of death in a house. This time he did knock. The woman came out to him, weeping, and said "Ah, Sir, if only you had been here last night. Last night my daughter was dying, now she is dead. But all yesterday evening she was longing, longing and saying—

" 'Oh, if I could see a priest! Oh that it would please God to send me a priest! Oh, I wish that a priest would come.' "

My husband did not keep Margery's letter with the other two stories, about the lectern and the cheque from India, and has now forgotten them; but he does remember that "Mr. Holmes" often related such experiences—they seem to have happened to him fairly frequently. In other ways he was apparently a very matter-of-fact person, who spent much of his time, especially when he was Archdeacon of London, looking after the spiritual welfare of trained nurses, about which no one seemed to have bothered very much at that time. To my regret I never met him; but I did know his sister, Mrs. Torr, who was married to another clergyman, Canon Torr—their daughters Gladys and Dona were friends of ours, and we stayed occasionally at their home, Carlett Park, near Eastham in Cheshire. Old Mrs. Torr was a completely *un*imaginative person—so unimaginative and unsuspecting that for several months during the first war she cheerfully harboured a German spy! Carlett Park lay near the western end of the Eastham ship canal; old Mrs. Torr, suddenly requiring a new lady's-maid, wrote to her accustomed servants' registry in London, and calmly accepted, on their recommendation, an allegedly Swiss maid. She made no particular enquiries; it never occurred to her as slightly suspicious that a German-speaking foreign maid should seek a post so conveniently placed for observing the movements of shipping. Fortunately her daughter Gladys was sharper. She had been away in the South when the new maid was engaged, and on her return home she resumed her custom of riding in the Park every morning before breakfast, and noticed with surprise that the Swiss woman made a habit of meeting the postman in the avenue and collecting her own letters from him—all the mail for the Park was normally brought up in one bag, which was opened, and the contents distributed by the butler, the postman taking away the outgoing mail in another bag. Gladys became suspicious, and on her return to London reported her suspicions in an appropriate quarter; enquiries were made, a watch was kept, and sure enough the excellent new maid was found to be a spy who had been "wanted" for some time; she was interned—greatly to old Mrs. Torr's dismay.

I mention this episode merely to emphasise the fact that the Holmes's, as a family, were not much given to flights of fancy.

Another example of precognition, rather similar to those of Archdeacon Holmes, I found not long since in an old diary of mine—the entry is dated 1 December 1914. It reads:

"Diana—our child—has whooping-cough; has had it since November the 16th. But Patty (her nurse, formerly mine) is so competent and experienced that I was confident that Diana would come through it easily, for she is a strong child, and over three months old; I was not at all anxious. On Sunday afternoon I coaxed Patty to go out for a walk. She came in after only half an hour—she had promised to stay out for an hour at least, and I was rather cross, and came down to the smoking-room in dudgeon. Less than five minutes later I heard her calling out, and ran up to the nursery. She was standing by the window holding Diana in her arms, with a finger in her mouth; the child was perfectly blue all over her face and head, and her little hands were bright blue; she was choking, but making no other sound. Patty said, 'Pull her tongue forward!—pull it forward!—keep it forward!' I tried to but couldn't, it was too slippery and too small. I tried to think why the tongue must be pulled forward, even as I told Patty that I couldn't; I thought of letting the air into the child's throat, and I slid my little finger along the roof of her mouth and pressed the tongue down and said—'Will it do if I keep her tongue down?'

Patty said, 'Yes—keep it down—keep her mouth open.' Patty was breathing like a runner with a bursting heart, and patting Diana's back. I asked if I should open the window; she nodded, and I threw it up with my left hand and we held Diana in front of it. Then the air seemed to come in with a sort of whistling sound, and Diana began to gasp, and then to cry, and Patty said—'She's getting better—she'll come round'—and she gave the little thing to me to hold and put her own finger in the tiny mouth. 'She was nearly gone,' Patty said, still panting. 'Oh, what a mercy I was in! Oh, what a mercy you were there! Another minute and she would have been gone.' All this time I was quite frozen with fright, and felt as if someone were holding my heart with cold hands, very tightly."

So much from the diary. The child recovered, but it was indeed a mercy that Patty had come in half an hour early. I should not have had the least idea what to do for the spasm which causes the tongue to be sucked back against the palate, which is what makes whooping-cough so deadly to small babies—so the doctor told us presently; the quick answer is chloroform, which relaxes the muscles, and he left a bottle with us.

Owen asked her why she came back so soon, since I had expressly said she was to be out for at least an hour? The grey-haired woman, who had had plenty of trouble with my temper as a child, replied, smiling a little, in her slight Buckinghamshire accent,—"Well, Sir, I was afraid Madam would be cross, but I wasn't easy about Baby, so I turned round and hurried home."

I am told that sometimes para-normal experiences come in the form of writing; I don't mean automatic writing, but just written messages. I have had no actual experience of this myself except to have a dream about it, many years ago, which I turned into a very successful short story; but I know one or two people to whom it has happened. I will give one example, which was told me by Lady Conesford, a sister of the late Robert Nichols, the poet.

As a young woman Anne Nichols had a rather close friend, who presently married a man called Charles Rutherford; to her regret he presently decided to settle in the Argentine and breed polo-ponies, which he did very successfully. The Rutherfords stayed out there for twenty-five years or more, but the friendship between the two women was maintained. At last, to Lady Conesford's considerable satisfaction, the Rutherfords returned to Europe; but presently they decided to settle in Ireland. From Ireland Mrs. Rutherford presently sent Lady Conesford a postcard, mentioning the places they were seeing, and so on; it did not call for any immediate answer, and Anne put it aside, as one does, to be dealt with some time; after three weeks or a month Mrs. Rutherford sent another postcard, again full of cheerful chat, but mildly reproaching her friend for not having replied to the earlier one. Guiltily—and again as one does—Anne went to her desk and looked out the first card, to see how long ago it was since she received it. Written across one end, at right angles to the rest of the writing, she saw the words—"Charles is dead". She was so shocked and upset that, unwisely, she tore up the card and threw it away. But Charles Rutherford *was* dead—he died very suddenly shortly after the second cheerful postcard was written; he was already dead by the time Anne Conesford went to her desk and looked out the original one.

Curious forms of precognition sometimes occur in dreams, it seems, as in the two instances which follow; and oddly enough both are concerned with an item in a newspaper.

Mrs. Bannerman, wife of Professor David Bannerman, the ornithologist, has kindly made me a present of the first. She dreamed one night (after her marriage) that she was going to be involved in a car smash three days later; the dream was so vivid that at breakfast the following morning, a Thursday, she related her dream and then pronounced firmly—"Nothing will induce me to get into a car on Sunday."

On the Sunday morning she picked up the newspaper; the first item that caught her eye was a paragraph announcing that a certain Winifred Holland (her own maiden name) of Cardiff (where she was born) had been killed in a car accident in Spain.

I find this a very curious one. Except for the name and the fact that both came from Cardiff, there was no link between Mrs. Bannerman and the dead woman—so why should she be as it were *visited* with this knowledge?—as if it concerned herself? However, as I have remarked before, the more pointless the paranormal experience, the more credible, to me.

The second precognition dream is almost equally pointless; it happened to my daughter Kate Willert quite recently. She and her husband were staying in the Pyrenees in their converted farmhouse, and she told him this dream over breakfast. I quote her letter:

"I was in bed on the terrace of a hospital, one of a long row of patients, with my right leg strung up as they do, with weights, on account of what presumably was a broken ankle—anyhow my ankle was in plaster; but I was cheerful and not in pain, chatting away with the others. We were on a broad terrace just above ground level, and below us was a big rather informal garden with a ha-ha at the bottom of it, and beyond a long sloping meadow ending at a beech-wood about 150 yards away. It was visiting-day, a hot sunny day, and all the visitors had brought their dogs to see the patients—I remember counting them. Paul (her husband) had brought Argos (their poodle) of course; there were also two golden spaniels, a fawn boxer bitch, a Jack Russell terrier, two long-haired dachshunds, a Dalmatian, and one or two more I can't identify now. Suddenly the whole doggy band stopped fooling about in the garden and went tearing off down the meadow, Argos in the lead, hunting—as he does in Richmond Park. Right down at the edge of the wood, he launched himself, barking, at what I had taken for a few small stakes of sun-dried wood, standing upright in the bright sunny grass—in a flash they all vanished, and Argos was left looking round with that ridiculous self-conscious air of frustration that he shows when squirrels dart up oak trees.

"I turned to Paul (the dream one) saying, 'Good Heavens! How extraordinary to see gophers in England! I've never seen them since I was a child, crossing Canada in the train.'

"The dream, or what I remember of it, ended there. I told it to the real-life Paul at breakfast at about eight forty-five, and he was amused, and recalled his own memories of the funny little creatures from America, and their lightning dashes into their burrows. At nine-thirty the papers arrived, and while he tackled *Le Monde*, I opened the *Sud-Ouest*. On an inner page I came on a paragraph recounting how in the new Parc National at our end of the Pyrenees the authorities, among their manifold tasks of organising and protecting it, had acquired from Switzerland a small colony of marmots, five females and three males, and had released them, hoping that they would propagate and flourish— since they were originally native to the Pyrenees, and only became extinct here about a hundred and fifty years ago. Marmots whistle an alarm before diving into their holes, and I don't think gophers do—my dream ones didn't; but as we say locally—'*C'est curieux tout de même, n'est-ce-pas?*'"

It is indeed—most curious. The gopher or prairie-dog and the marmot belong to slightly different *genera*; but both live in colonies in burrows, both dash underground for shelter when alarmed, and they are so alike in appearance and general behaviour that one species of prairie-dog is called, in the United States, "the Louisiana Marmot".

The business of Lady Conesford's postcard struck me particularly because of the dream I had, years ago, on which my short story, *The Accident*, was based. In the dream two rather disagreeable English climbers (disagreeable because they were boastful, pushing and unscrupulous) had been killed in an accident near Zermatt, where I and my brother Jack were staying; in the dream we went to their funeral. Soon after it I was startled and then alarmed to get a series of postcards from the dead men from Italy, saying that they were coming to Zermatt and hoped to climb with us. Each successive card was from a place nearer to Zermatt, till finally one arrived saying "Zermatt tonight"—it was brought down by hand from the Regina Margherita hut on Monte Rosa (here crossed by the Italian frontier) by some guides. This final card frightened me out of my wits. In my panic I showed the whole series of postcards to Dr. Anthony Rolleston (in real life a member of the Alpine Club and a psychologist, who worked at a looney-bin somewhere in the home counties) and asked his advice. He said the writing on the cards was undoubtedly that of one of the dead men, and that their intention was evident; no longer having bodies of their own to climb with, they wished to possess us and climb with ours. But he promised to take care of us —he made us pack our rucksacks and took us up to the Trift hut, where, after supper, he gave us a lot of aspirins and put us to bed upstairs; he said he would stay awake downstairs to guard our bodies, and that as soon as we were asleep he would put our souls in his pocket-book, where they would be quite safe. In my dream this ridiculous solution satisfied me perfectly, and I woke up quite happy; but the horror of the arrival, in my dream, day after day, of those postcards from two dead men made a deep impression, and years later, when I was well launched on writing, I used the dream as the basis of a short story with a tragic ending.

Oddly, for a story with such a highly improbable plot, it had a remarkable success. It is normal enough for novels to be translated into foreign languages—mine have been published, first and last, in sixteen different ones—but rather unusual for short stories, except those of authors with immense reputations, like Hemingway or Maugham; yet over the years *The Accident* has been translated into four or five European languages—into French actually twice.

In fact many of my short stories have a supernatural element, and are based on dreams. The very first of all, *The Buick Saloon*, about a second-hand car haunted by the voices of a former owner and her lover, owed its existence to a dream about a haunted car in Peking. I was fortunate in getting this one, and most of its successors, published in the States; American magazines pay two or three times as much for a short story as English ones. But my literary agents, both in London and New York, warned me that ghost-stories were not popular in America, in fact there was a strong prejudice against them—they begged me to write more ordinary ones, and I did manage to achieve several. But the dream-based ones, with a supernatural element, came much more easily to me.

I have often wondered about this American dislike of ghost-stories—which I believe to be a fact—and what its origin may be. Is it that so much of the country has only been inhabited for such a short time, relatively speaking?—that the soil of a land needs to be watered with blood and enriched with corpses for ghosts to flourish there? Or did the matter-of-fact Puritanism of the founding fathers, which has so coloured the whole American outlook, discourage the idea of ghosts? Certainly I never heard any ghost-stories in New England, whereas in Louisiana there seemed to be plenty going about—Louisiana, with its long Spanish and French occupations, is so much more European in outlook and feeling than most of the rest of the States. The little pockets of Greeks and Poles in the manufacturing towns of New England have not in any marked way affected the cultural *climate* of the North-east coast; while the Indians—who surely had a strong belief in the spirits of the dead?—have left little or nothing behind them but their enchanting place-names.

I wish I knew about this. One cannot speak of a *racial* attitude or atmosphere in connection with a country of such mixed ethnic origins as the United States, and indeed, I believe it is unfashionable among modern anthropologists to think in terms of "racial characteristics" at all. (This seems to me rather absurd: if one lives for some time in two adjoining countries like Portugal and Spain, for instance, no normally observant person can fail to be struck by the difference in the character and outlook of the inhabitants the moment he crosses the frontier.) Certainly in parts of the world where racial origins are fairly distinct, the attitude towards the supernatural varies very much from one racial group to another— as witness the prevalence of second sight in the West Highlands, and its almost total absence in, say, Yorkshire, Devonshire or Surrey.

PART VII

Second Sight

Second Sight

No intelligent and well-educated person now doubts, I suppose, the existence of second sight in the West Highlands—at least no one who has ever lived there for any length of time—and few such people could fail to be struck by the all-round closeness to, really the familiarity with, the supernatural in the mental climate of the Highlanders. I first came into contact with all this in 1906, when my father rented a small shooting lodge, Kilcheran, on Lismore from the old Duke of Argyll, and we spent three months there. In 1911 we spent another three months at Tavool, in Mull, and after my marriage in 1913, I spent many weeks every year at Skipness in Argyll with Owen's cousins the Grahams; later I extended my knowledge by prolonged sailing trips to the Outer Hebrides on *Frolic*, Professor Sir Geoffrey Taylor, O.M.'s, yacht, and by archaeological expeditions on my own account, and visits to friends as far afield as Inverness-shire and Wester Ross. First and last, for the better part of sixty years I have been in and out of the Highlands, and this peculiar mental climate has become quite familiar to me. But that does not diminish its peculiarity to someone born an Anglo-Saxon.

The first impact, during those three months on Lismore, was strong. I was in my teens, an impressionable age, and the circumstances were favourable. There was nothing to do at Kilcheran but a little rough shooting, and some modest trout fishing in two lochs—and the sailing. The great stroke of good fortune for us lay in the personality of one of the two men whose large chunky fishing-boat my father had hired for the whole summer, to be at our disposal, with them as crew, to take us out sailing whenever and wherever we wished to go. John and Duncan Black were the sons of a famous character, Donald Black, known as Donal Daunsher, Donald the Dancer—before the advent of Macbrayne's steamers he had sailed the Lismore packet, the island's one link with the mainland, to and fro to Oban across Loch Linnhe, carrying mails, passengers, and general cargo. He had been not only a brilliant dancer, but a renowned singer and teller of stories, as well as a poet in his own right—he made both verses and tunes for local occasions, and a poem had been made about him himself, in Gaelic, of which the sense of the chorus was roughly—

Oh Donal the Dancer comes sailing very fast,
So fast that the mast of his boat is bent with the wind.
If he gets a dram or two with old Angus [an Oban publican]
He'll dance you a figure on the pavement!

Donal the Dancer had been considered a slightly disreputable character, owing to this habit of drinking drams and subsequently dancing "figures" (the word used in the original Gaelic) in the open street; both the sons, in consequence, were strict teetotallers. But John Black had remembered practically all his father's songs and stories, and during the long days which we spent sailing up and down Loch Linnhe in the *Mary Black*, he poured them out to us. Every ruined castle, every bay and headland, had its story attached to it, often several stories, and one or more songs as well; John would sing the songs in Gaelic, and then give us the words in his own beautiful direct translation, as he did the stories—I heard all about the Appin murder from him long before ever I read of it in Stevenson. I realise now, too late, how almost criminally wrong I was not to have written down these stories before I forgot them; some of the songs I do still remember, in Gaelic—John always made me learn the Gaelic words, and then taught me, most carefully, *how* to sing them, with the proper stress and emphasis; for the airs he would often pull out his chanter (the part of the bagpipes that carries the melody) and play it over and over, till I had that by heart too.

There were one or two ghost-stories attaching to the many old castles round about, but I don't recall any that referred specifically to second sight. What I did learn, though, was the enormous importance attached to good and ill luck. It was unlucky if a hare actually *crossed* your path, though seeing one in a field did not matter; when going fishing it was very unlucky to meet a woman on the road—if she spoke to you you might as well give up and go home. I have known John Black do this; he and Duncan used to fish at night sometimes, when their responsibilities to us were over for the day. When we learned how seriously they took this business of meeting a woman, my sisters and I would scramble over the low stone walls bordering the road if we saw John's bulky blue-clad figure, with the greying red beard, approaching in the distance, and pretend to pick flowers till he was safely past.

One supernatural thing we did hear about at first hand on Lismore, and that was the minister's elemental. The Established church on the island was at Clachan, at the northern end, some seven miles away; of course there were no cars then, only the horse-drawn carts known as "machines", and my father had what we young ones regarded as the very unfortunate idea of inviting the minister to come down on Sunday afternoons to conduct a service and preach in the billiard-room at Kilcheran and stay to tea, so that both we and all the people at our end of the island could perform our religious devotions without a fourteen-mile walk. (In 1906 really strict Presbyterians would not take a horse out on the Sabbath, even if they had a horse to take, which most of them hadn't—this notion of our father's was as popular with the locals as it was deplored by us.) But this meant that we saw a lot of the Minister, a gentle, humble grey-haired man, whose wife, we learned, was an invalid; my mother thought at first that this was the cause of his general air of fatigue and depression, though he generally forced himself to make cheerful conversation.

However, my mother usually got people's confidence sooner rather than later, and it so happened that I was stitting with them in the drawing-room at Kilcheran when he told her of his trouble. It was, he said, an elemental—and I have never forgotten the horrifying matter-of-factness with which he described the things it did. He had recently managed to get a clinical thermometer sent from Glasgow, with which to take his wife's temperature; they were both delighted with it. But one evening as it lay, out of its case, on the table by the bed, suddenly they saw it rise, "flash against the ceiling"—I remember his very words—before it fell to the floor and was smashed to pieces. (This happened during our visit.) On another occasion the maid had just carried a scuttle of coals upstairs and left it on the landing before taking it into the bedroom; the minister, standing in the hall below, found himself being pelted with lumps of coal, though the scuttle was in full view, with no one near it—the hall of course was soon in an awful mess. Neither he nor his wife suffered any serious physical injury —the actions were mostly trivial, silly and spiteful; but the effect on her health of never knowing whether they would have an undisturbed night's rest or not was most serious. The thing came at all hours, but more by night than by day, and having turned the lamp out they would lie awake, listening; when it was coming the dogs at the farms down the road would begin to howl—far away at first, then at each farm, nearer and nearer, till by the glimmer of the night-light—they dared not sleep in the dark—they would see her hair-brush rise off the dressing-table and drop into the water-jug on the washstand, or fly across and hit the minister on the face.

What, for him, made the affliction even more penitential was his conviction that he was being visited with this terrible trial as a punishment for some sin. I didn't hear him say that; he told my mother so on another occasion, and she told me—it distressed her very much. She did not believe either in the sin on his part, nor that such a punishment had been meted out by Providence, especially to the innocent wife. If an account of Borley Rectory had already been published by then, we did not know of it; this whole affair was new to us, and wholly mysterious. But my mother thought that it amply accounted for the wife's ill-health, and in this she proved to be right. Six years later, when I was working in London, I went up and spent my summer holiday on Lismore, staying as a p.g. with Mrs. Shankland, the farmer's wife, at Kilcheran—of course I enquired after the minister. He had died, she said, four years previously. And his wife? I have always remembered with rather wry amusement the reply I received.

"Och, she's fine. She picked up wonderful since himself was laid away. I've known it go the same way with many a one, many a time."

Second sight is generally supposed, by those who concern themselves with these matters, to be most prevalent in the Islands and the remoter places, but we were interested to learn presently that it exists, and is believed in, in relatively sophisticated parts of the Highlands, and by well-educated people. Some time after that first visit to Lismore my sister Therèse went up to stay with a friend whom she had met when working for the Lady Almoner of St. Thomas's Hospital; this friend's aunt, a Mrs. Fletcher, lived on the outskirts of Oban, in surroundings considered locally to be positively metropolitan. Mrs. Fletcher's house stood near the seashore; on the morning after my sister's arrival her hostess, waking early (actually about 5 a.m.) looked out of her window and saw Therèse walking on the shore. This struck her as something so incredible that she instantly assumed that she was seeing a phantasm, and that it foreboded my sister's death; she passed the next two hours in great distress, till on going to the bathroom as usual at seven o'clock she encountered Thérèse on the stairs, her hair wind-blown, her boots covered with indubitable sand. Infinitely relieved, Mrs. Fletcher took her bath; later, when they had made friends, and she had become accustomed to my sister's habit of matutinal walks, she admitted to her fears, and explained that to see a phantasm of a person generally means that he or she will die fairly soon.

Premonitions are not only visual; sounds are also thought to forebode future events, sometimes with inconvenient practical results. I heard a good example of this in 1928 when I was staying at Morar Lodge with the late Professor Caldwell and his wife, rubbing interlace ornament on tombstones in the neighbourhood. I learned that there was a good stone or a cross-shaft, I am no longer sure which, in a graveyard up one of the neighbouring sea-lochs, and my host kindly arranged for a man in Mallaig, who had a powerful motor-boat, to take me to the place, and drove me in to meet him. It was a longish distance, and a pouring wet day, very unfavourable for rubbing stones; however, all the arrangements had been made, and I could at least measure and describe the stone, so of course I went.

One of the things my early experiences on Lismore had taught me was that the proper way to pass the time in a boat is telling stories or singing songs; but it is not always easy for a stranger, especially from England, to persuade the Highlander to embark on these activities. However, if the stranger himself volunteers to sing a song in Gaelic, the ice is quickly broken; thanks to John Black's lessons I could do this, and presently my elderly boatman and I, in our dripping oilskins, with a sail over our knees, were launched on a regular *ceilidh* (an entertainment, part concert, part recitations). Better still, he came from Barrà, which I already knew fairly well, and we were able to exchange gossip about various Barrà characters, like the priest, and the postmaster at

North Bay (known locally as the Coddie). And finally he told me this story.

A man in Barrà, a relation of his, bought a new fishing-boat, and kept her down at Castlebay; but noises were heard in her, the tramp of feet, and knocking and hammering—this was thought to sound like making a coffin, and was regarded as so ominous that the owner could not get paid hands to sail in her, and had to scrape together a crew from among his relatives, of whom my boatman, as quite a young man, was one. They had a gun on board to shoot seagulls, to get feathers for tying the white flies, used for catching ling—they would fish with the lines when the herring were not about; and one day out at sea another young boy in the crew had an accident with the gun, and wounded himself seriously. They laid him down and wrapped him up, and the boat's owner asked him presently—"My poor boy, how are you feeling now?" He replied—"Oh, the cold, the cold! T'is coming up my legs to my body." So they boiled a kettle in the cabin, and dipped strips of blanket in the hot water, and wrung them out, and wrapped them round his legs to warm him. They sailed back to Castlebay, tied up at the quay, and sent for the doctor; on his orders, to get the youth ashore they took off the cabin door and improvised a stretcher by nailing it on to two spars. The onlookers on the quay heard the hammering, and the noise of feet running to and fro; the boy was taken ashore and died. "And after that, any man at all would sail in her"—that was how my boatman's tale ended. The impending disaster had happened, so now the boat was all right.

A much shorter and slightly different version of this story was noted down in 1896 by Father Allan McDonald, a priest who worked in South Uist and on the island of Eriskay for twenty-one years, till his death in 1905; it was printed in 1968 in *Strange Things*, a book by Dr. John Campbell of Canna and Trevor Hall. Fr. Allan, a rather remarkable person, was deeply interested in folklore, and made a considerable collection of folk tales, including fifty-eight concerning second sight; all of these fifty-eight are printed in *Strange Things*—which was Fr. Allan's own title for this particular volume, really a quarto note-book, of his various collections of folk-lore. The dates fitted all right; my boatman was an elderly man, and no one who knows the oral memory of the Highlander would be surprised at his recalling words spoken thirty-three years before.

This section of Dr. Campbell's book is a mine of interest for the enquirer into second sight, though the stories as printed are told so laconically as to make little impression on anyone unfamiliar with Highland modes of thought and speech, and indeed with the way of life in the Highlands as late as the close of the nineteenth century. The English reader, learning that John Morrison was playing the bagpipes before the fire in his house on a snowy winter's evening, when "the cock came down from the roost and began to crow and to leap up, flapping his wings at the piper", is liable to be so startled at the idea of the cock sharing his master's living-room as to be less impressed than he is meant to be by the instant conviction of Morrison's wife that the bird's agitation foreboded some death or disaster—so much so that she bade her husband cease his playing. She was in the right of it; not long after that same night the priest knocked on the door, bringing the news that Morrison's brother had perished in the snow.

In fact poultry normally roosted at the farther end of the big room, kitchen and living-room combined, where all the life of the house was carried on; often there were boxed-in beds against the walls at the end nearest the hearth, such as one may still see today in the remoter parts of Ireland. And a disturbance among the poultry for which no obvious cause was evident was regularly regarded as a portent.

English readers, again, might be puzzled by the references to the lid of a box or trunk "in the room" opening of itself, some days or weeks *before* an article was taken from it for use in connection with a death—in one case recorded by Fr. Allan a towel was later taken out to be used at the time of washing a corpse. Why, the sophisticated southerner asks himself, have an unlocked trunk in the living-room? The answer of course is that in the Outer Islands the people had very little furniture; clothes normally hung from pegs in the walls, and small objects of every description were housed in the trunk—and since there was nowhere to keep it but in the living-room, the movement of the lid, without human agency, was observed—often by several people at once. Also, the skin from which the bag of the bag-pipes was formed, when not attached to the pipe, was sometimes left lying by itself on a bed or on the lid of the said trunk; the pipes were invariably played at funerals, and if the skin bag "groaned aloud" when so lying, untouched, it portended a death. Fr. Allan gives two instances of this.

All these disjointed stories must seem very trivial, and in themselves they often are. All the small things of everyday life are involved in the Highlander's experience of second sight—perhaps understandably among people to whom the invisible world is as real and as omnipresent as the visible one. But it should be emphasised that no one *likes* having second sight, especially in the numerous instances of seeing phantasms of the living when they are known to be hundreds of miles distant; this power of "seeing" is never voluntary, let alone deliberately sought. It is regarded rather as a trial, to be borne with resignation.

Conclusion

These rather random experiences of extra-sensory perception, either my own personal ones, or at first-hand from reliable people in my immediate circle, when thus assembled together seem, to me, to lead towards one conclusion, and to raise one or two questions. I cannot, myself, escape the conclusion that in all these different manifestations of para-normal experiences, whether passively undergone—as in apparitions, dreams, "knowings", telepathic experiences or second sight; or deliberately pursued— as in water-divining, graphology, tumbler-pushing and telepathic experiments—one single faculty is involved, and that, a faculty closely related to the subconscious. The fact that in a given individual only some, and not all the various aspects of what I call the "faculty" emerge does not seem to me to invalidate this theory; it does not surprise me that I, who passively experience knowings and veridical dreams, and can also actively practise graphology, should be incapable of water-divining, and noticeably poor at telepathic experiments; while Frances Graham, a highly successful dowser and particularly good at telepathy never, to my knowledge, had either knowings or veridical dreams. It also seems to me highly probable that human beings share this general "faculty" with animals, at least as far as the passive experience of being aware of apparitions is concerned, and that in them it is more highly developed than in us—witness Lord

Granville's dogs' and our ponies' reactions to something imperceptible by human beings.

That is as far as one can take it, with animals, and it is not of course susceptible of proof—though anyone who has actually had a horse suddenly shy violently under him at something totally invisible and inaudible is rather likely not to worry very much about scientific proof!

One question which arises, for me anyhow, is whether it is a fact that what I have called the supra-normal faculty is really latent in all human beings?—and more in some ethnic groups than in others? Certainly in Britain second sight would seem to be much more in evidence among people with Highland blood than among the rest of us. And have gypsies really got some special gift in the matter of reading character from hands, and foretelling the future?—or have they developed it by constant practice? They, I suppose, are one of the most clearly defined of ethnic groups. And if the faculty is to some extent latent in all human beings, does it diminish with progressive mechanisation and urbanisation? Certainly second-sight in the Highlands is much more noticeable among those living in remote places, and I am told—though I have no personal or first-hand knowledge on this—that this is also the case among African tribes. On the other hand water-divining is successfully practised by town-dwellers, as e.g. Mr. Comley, the Swindon plumber, while Frances Graham had spent nearly as much of her life in Cambridge and London as in Argyll when I saw her at work with the hazel rod. And if the faculty is latent in all human beings, how is it related to "the collective unconscious of mankind", posited by Professor Jung, or Sir Aleister Hardy's similar theory of a group-mind of the species,[1] building itself up from conscious or sub-conscious human experience down the ages? Both these concepts seem to fit the facts so far as they are yet understood, which admittedly is not very far; and the power of

[1] See *The Hidden Springs*, by Renée Haynes.

human experience to modify the "collective unconscious" throws a startling light on some theological conceptions such as the Fall, and the importance of the purely spiritual work of contemplative orders.

It seems to me that there is a lot of most interesting work still to be done on all this: by recording and collating the distribution of the various manifestations of the para-normal faculty, the answers to these questions might gradually emerge. I should be very happy if this book encouraged some readers, at least, to *trust* any such experiences of their own, to record them carefully, and to exchange them with others. People seem often to be timid and even nervous about such experiences; they tend to shy away from them—which means the loss of potentially valuable material concerning a deeply interesting and important subject.